The Founding of the Kashmir State

The Founding of the Kashmir State

A biography of Maharajah Gulab Singh 1792-1858

K. M. Panikkar

GYAN

Published by

GYAN

Gyan Publishing House
5, Ansari Road
Daryaganj, New Delhi-110002
Phone: 011-47034999, 9811692060
E-mail: books@gyanbooks.com

Distribution Network
gyanbooks.com
India, USA, Canada, UK, Australia

ISBN: 978-81-212-7031-1 (HB)
First Published, 1930

2nd Impression 2024

Printed at: Gyan Press, Delhi.

The Founding of the Kashmir State
Author: K. M. PANIKKAR

Dutta, Kashmir

THE MAHARAJA SHRI GULAB SINGH

K. M. PANIKKAR

The Founding of the Kashmir State

A BIOGRAPHY OF
MAHARAJAH GULAB SINGH
1792-1858

PREFACE

THIS short memoir, in which I have traced the life story of Maharajah Gulab Singh, is meant to fill a gap in the history of India in the nineteenth century. Gulab Singh's name is known to students of Indian history only as an overgrown feudatory of the Lahore kingdom, who, taking advantage of the confusion which followed the death of Ranjit Singh, was able to carve out a State for himself. The establishment of the Jammu and Kashmir State by the treaty of 1846, and its recognition later in the century as one of the great internal States of India, have obscured the essential greatness of Gulab Singh as a soldier and a statesman. His claim to high rank in the roll of Indian statesmen was established firmly even before he became the ruler of Kashmir. When he was in his thirties he had attained eminence in the Court of Ranjit Singh as an intrepid general and a far-seeing statesman. When Ranjit Singh died in 1839, Gulab Singh was easily the most influential personage in the Sikh Empire and was its chief feudatory. In the years that followed (1840-1842) he conquered Baltistan and Western Tibet, and added to the geographical boundaries of India an area such as no ruler in the past had ever done.

Even if Gulab Singh had died before the Treaty of Amritsar had guaranteed to him his State of Jammu and transferred to him the Sikh rights in Kashmir and its dependencies, he would have been justly regarded as one of the most remarkable men of his time in India. It is, therefore, as a contribution to the history of India, and not as a chapter in the history of Jammu and Kashmir, that this work is offered.

There has been no lack of original material for this memoir. The main authority on which the life of Gulab Singh could be based is the contemporary record entitled *Gulabnama,* written in Persian, by Dewan Kirpa Ram, the Maharajah's private secretary and the son of Dewan Jwala Sahai, the Maharajah's Prime Minister. This work, though written in the flowery style of the Persian panegyrists, is none the less a remarkable historical document, as the Dewan published in it many original documents which are not now available elsewhere. Its facts and chronology are beyond dispute. The Dewan was also fully conversant with the political conditions of the Punjab at the time, and his descriptions of events are vivid and informed by direct knowledge of men and things.

Three other histories, two written in Dogri, the local dialect, and one in Urdu, also deal with the life of Gulab Singh. They are not of much value, though I have been able to gather from them stray facts relating to the family of Gulab Singh and his early life.

The English authorities on the period which deal with events narrated in the book are numerous. A few of the most important are mentioned below:

Life of Henry Lawrence. By Edwardes and Merivale. (Smith Elder, Third Edition, London, 1873.)

The Punjab. By Lieut.-Colonel Steinbach. (London, 1845.)

Court and Camp of Ranjit Singh. By the Hon. W. G. Osborne. (London, Henry Colburn, 1840.)

Thirty-five Years in the East. By Dr. Martin Honigberger. (H. Balture, London, 1852.)

Ladak. By Alexander Cunningham. (W. H. Allen and Co., London, 1854.)

History of the Reigning Family of Lahore, with some account of the Jammu Rajahs. By G. C. Smyth. (Thacker and Co., Calcutta, 1847.)

History of the Sikhs. By J. D. Cunningham. (Murray, London, 1849.)

Punjab Government Records.

Lahore Political Diaries, Vols. III., IV., V., and VI.

All these books are more or less contemporary, and their authors were in most cases men who took part in the Punjab politics of the time. Captain Cunningham, the historian of the Sikhs, was assistant to the Agent to the Governor-General at Ludhiana. He was the officer selected to go to Tibet in order to witness the evacuation of Lhassa territories by Zorawar Singh. Alexander Cunningham, the historian of the Ladak campaign, was sent by agreement between Gulab Singh and the Company to fix the frontier between Ladak and Tibet. Edwardes, the biographer of Sir Henry Lawrence, is no other than Lieutenant Edwardes, the brilliant young political officer attached to Sir Henry at Lahore in 1846-1848. Steinbach was an officer of Ranjit Singh. Honigberger was the State physician to the Lahore Court, and was a friend of the Jammu family.

Contemporary histories, though they have great value from an historical point of view, undoubtedly possess one disadvantage, especially when they are written by persons who have taken an active part in the affairs they narrate. Not merely do they adopt a partisan attitude, but they allow their judgments of men and matters to be clouded by violent prejudices. One has only to read the contemporary biographies of such men as Napoleon. Gulab Singh has been no exception to this. He was traduced, slandered, and openly accused in his lifetime by the champions of the Sikhs, by the imperialists and annexationists of the day, and by the anonymous writers in the Press, to whom his towering personality offered a unique target for attack. But an impartial investigation of the facts cannot fail to establish the greatness of Gulab Singh both as a man and a statesman.

K. M. PANIKKAR

DELHI

CONTENTS

CHAPTER I

EARLY DAYS

THE hilly tract which lies between the sunny plains of the Punjab and the pleasant Valley of Kashmir and now forms the Province of Jammu was never before the time of Gulab Singh united under any single ruler. From Sialkot in British territory the plain rises in gradual ascent, and within a few miles becomes hilly and ragged. The lower Himalayan ranges begin of a sudden behind the town of Jammu, which, placed on a slope of over 1,300 feet, overlooks and commands the plain watered by the Chenab and the Ravi. These hills, which become higher and higher in the interior and cut up the country into isolated and inaccessible areas, formed a succession of ramparts behind which the local inhabitants safeguarded their independence and lived a life of placid contentment unaffected by the changes and revolutions in Hindustan.

The ruling classes of this hilly tract were Rajputs, who seem to have taken refuge in these mountain fastnesses when the Rajput hegemony in the Punjab was shattered in the twelfth century by the invasion of Mohammad of Ghor. Their petty principalities, the most important of which were those of Jammu,

Khistwar, and Bhadarwah, maintained their independence even during the Moghul times, though no doubt they paid a nominal tribute and accepted the overlordship of the Padishah of Hindustan. On the disintegration of the Moghul kingdom in the first half of the eighteenth century, following the invasion of Nadir Shah, the Rajput rulers who held sway around the town of Jammu regained their complete independence. They even acquired under Rajah Dhrov Deo and his son, Rajah Ranjit Deo, some prominence in the politics of the Northern Punjab. Ranjit Deo was a ruler who was highly respected in the hilly tracts over which he held sway. He received a jagir from the Durranni king for sending a small force to Kashmir *viâ* Banihal to punish Rajah Sukh Tewan. He subdued most of the petty hill rajahs around Jammu, notably Nihar Singh, Rajah of Khistwar; Shamsher Chand, Rajah of Chenani; Kirchipal, Rajah of Bhadarwah; and Amrit Pal, Rajah of Besolhi. He also held many jagirs in the Punjab, especially in the district of Gujerat. But this independence which Ranjit Deo achieved was short-lived. With the breakdown of Mohammadan authority in the Punjab the great Sikh misls began to acquire political and territorial importance, and Jammu, along with the rest of the Northern Punjab, became the scene of rivalry between the sardars of the Bhangi, Kaneihya, and

Sukerchakia misls. The sardars of the Bhangi misl attacked Jammu in about 1770 and compelled Ranjit Deo to pay tribute to them.

Ranjit Deo had two sons, Brij Lal and Dulel Singh. Brij Lal revolted against his father and sought the help of Charrat Singh, the Sukerchakia chief, and together they attacked Jammu. Ranjit Deo naturally depended for help upon the Bhangi chief whose overlordship he had accepted. In the fight that took place at Jammu, Charrat Singh was killed. The Sukerchakia partisans, fearing that Janda Singh, the Bhangi chief, might profit by this catastrophe, had him also murdered.

Brij Lal, who succeeded his father in 1780, was a great friend of Mahan Singh, the son of Charrat Singh, who is known to history as the father of Ranjit Singh. Brij Lal now considered himself strong enough to claim from the Bhangi chieftains some of his estates which had fallen to them and to reassert his independence. The Bhangis secured the help of the Kaneihya misl, and in the fight that followed Mahan Singh was defeated and Brij Lal had to agree to a humiliating peace, by which he undertook to pay a tribute to the Kaneihya chieftain. On the pretext that this tribute had fallen into arrears, the Kaneihya chieftain decided to attack Jammu. He requested the help of Mahan Singh in this expedition.

Mahan Singh, though he had vowed solemn vows of friendship with Brij Lal, forgot his obligations and agreed to help. But one who was not loyal even to his own sworn friend was not likely to be faithful to a temporary alliance. Before the Kaneihya chieftain began to march, Mahan Singh attacked Jammu, sacked the town and plundered the treasure accumulated in the palace. Laden with the booty he retired to the plains, leaving Brij Lal Deo to the government of his principality. The sack of Jammu saved its independence for a time. The contending Sikh chieftains, knowing that there was nothing left in the treasury, left Jammu well alone. The sovereignty of the House of Dhrov Deo over the surrounding country disappeared, but Brij Lal was still in possession of the Jammu town and fort and continued to maintain the form and court of petty royalty. The hilly districts of the interior remained in the possession of the other members of the family, who held them as jagirs. On the death of Brij Lal, he was succeeded by his one-year-old child Sampurna Deo. The State was managed by Mian Mota, a cousin of Brij Lal. Sampurna Deo died at the age of eleven, and was succeeded by Jeet Singh, the son of Dulel Singh.

Gulab Singh is descended in direct line from Rajah Dhrov through his third son, Mian Soorut Deo. Soorut Deo, who was thus the third brother of Rajah Ranjit Deo, had a son, Mian Zorawar Singh. His son was Kishore Singh, who held the jagir of Andarwah in Jammu Tehsil. Gulab Singh was his eldest son. The following is the genealogy of the family:

- Dhrov Deo
  - Ranjit Deo
    - Brij Lal Deo (expelled from throne, 1780, by Mahan Singh)
    - Dulel Singh
      - Jeet Singh
  - Ghunsar Deo
  - Soorut Deo
    - Mian Mota (assassinated)
    - Zorawar Singh
      - Kishore Singh
        - GULAB SINGH
          - Randhir Singh
          - Sohan Singh
          - Ranbir Singh
        - Dhyan Singh
          - Hira Singh
          - Jawahir Singh
          - Moti Singh of Poonch
        - Suchet Singh
    - Dulla Bhoola
  - Bulwant Deo

Some doubt was cast on the genealogy of the Jammu family by Cunningham and others, whose enthusiastic admiration of the Sikhs led them to an unreasonable hatred of Rajah Gulab Singh, whom they considered to be the chief cause of the ruin of the Sikh State. But there is no doubt whatever about the genealogy of the family. Zorawar Singh was alive during a considerable portion of Maharajah Ranjit Singh's reign, and Mian Kishore Singh, the father of Gulab Singh, was also later on at the

Lahore Court. Maharajah Ranjit Singh, in his grant of the Raj of Jammu to Gulab Singh, mentions the fact of Gulab's ancestors having been the rulers of the State. Ranjit Singh's father and grandfather had fought against the Rajahs of Jammu, Ranjit Deo and Brij Lal Deo, and therefore knew the history of that family intimately. The ancestry of Maharajah Gulab Singh became a matter of controversy, not only through the malice of his enemies, but also through the sycophancy of his courtiers. A Kashmiri Pandit went to the length of identifying the thirty-five missing kings in Kalhanas' list of Kashmir kings in the Rajataranjini with the early ancestors of the Jammu family.[1] There is, however, not the least doubt that Gulab Singh was descended in the direct male line from Rajah Dhrov Deo, the Rajput prince of the Surya Vansi (Solar) dynasty, who ruled over Jammu in the eighteenth century.

Mian Kishore Singh is reported to have been a valiant soldier. He lived mainly on his jagir at Andarwah, eight miles from the modern town of Samba. His financial condition does not seem to have been prosperous, and he achieved distinction only after his sons attained prominence. Kishore Singh married a Rajput lady of the Jij caste. The

[1] P. 73, foot-note to Stein's edition of *Rajataranjini*. (Constable, London.)

marriage was celebrated at Gam Madtha, a village in the Besolhi district. By this lady he had three sons, Gulab Singh, Dhyan Singh, and Suchet Singh.

Gulab Singh was born in 1792 (on the 5th Katik, 1849, Vikrami Samvat), Dhyan Singh was born in 1796, and Suchet Singh in 1801. Early in his childhood Gulab Singh was sent to live with his grandfather, Zorawar Singh, a stern old warrior who lived in his jagir, Dyawago, at some distance from Jammu. Like all true Rajputs of the time, Zorawar Singh had great contempt for the study of letters, and does not seem to have taken any trouble to give his grandson a literary education. All that Gulab Singh seems to have learnt was to read and write. But though Zorawar neglected to give Gulab Singh any school education, he trained him in all manly arts. Thus even at a very early age Gulab Singh could ride his horse like any cavalry trooper and wield his sword with deadly effect. He was also an excellent marksman.

An opportunity soon came for Gulab Singh to exhibit his prowess. The affairs of Jammu were in great confusion. Rajah Jeet Singh, the nephew of Brij Lal Deo, was an incompetent man, and his rani was an ambitious, intriguing woman. She took the management of affairs in her own hands. Taking advantage of the confusion resulting from this, Ranjit Singh ordered, in 1808, Bhai Hukam

Singh to reduce Jammu and to annex it to the Sikh State. The Sikh general advanced with a very considerable force and reached the confines of Jammu. Mian Mota, who was in charge of the defence, organised a small force and came out of the town to give battle. When the forces met outside the Gumat Gate, young Gulab Singh, who was but a boy of sixteen, was found taking an active and prominent part in the battle. His spirit of adventure had been roused. Here was a unique opportunity to distinguish himself before his Rajput brethren and to earn a name for himself. Without even obtaining permission from his grandfather, Gulab Singh borrowed a charger from the stables and appeared on the battlefield. His prowess on that day attracted the attention of Hukam Singh, the enemy commander. The defence was to some extent successful, and Gulab Singh's part in it was no mean one. Hukam Singh had to withdraw his forces to Saidgarh. But a skirmish could not stem the onrush of Ranjit Singh's forces, and the whole province passed under the suzerainty of Ranjit Singh and the Lahore government.

Soon after this Gulab Singh left his grandfather's protection. It seems that one day he took a horse from his grandfather's stable and went for a ride in the forest. By careless riding he hurt the animal, and on return his grandfather, who, true to his soldier's creed, loved his horse as a comrade, scolded the boy for his carelessness. The sensitive mind of the boy—he was still hardly more than seventeen—was so hurt by these unkind words that he took some ornaments from his mother and left the house at night with a few attendants. His original idea was to enlist in the army of Shah Shuja, the unlucky ruler of Kabul, whom his uncle, Shah Mahmud, had expelled from Afghanistan and succeeded on the Kabul throne with the help of the Bakarzai tribe. But when he reached the Indus his attendants refused to go to Afghanistan.

Foiled in his intention to go to Kabul, Gulab Singh approached Dewan Khushwaqt Rai, who was managing the jagir of Sardar Nehal Singh of Attari. The Dewan was intensely disliked by the people of the jagir, whom he oppressed greatly by his merciless exactions. As there was great unrest among them, the Dewan decided to raise a small force for the purpose of defending himself and his master's property. Gulab Singh approached the Dewan and offered his services, which were accepted. He is himself responsible for the story that a certain jamadar, who was formerly in the employ of Zorawar Singh, reported to Khushwaqt Rai the identity of the new recruit. Gulab Singh did not have to wait long to win his spurs. Soon after he joined service a skirmish occurred in which the Dewan's forces were routed by the villagers, who attacked the fort itself. It was only Gulab Singh's courage and intrepid action that saved the fort and enabled the Dewan to put down the incipient rebellion.

This action of his attracted attention, and Hukam Singh, who already had occasion to notice the young Mian's prowess, reported the matter to Ranjit Singh. Ranjit Singh asked Mian Mota to send Gulab Singh down to him. In Samvat 1867 (A.D. 1809) Gulab Singh joined the army of Ranjit Singh at Daska, a village a few miles from Sialkot.

CHAPTER II

GULAB SINGH AT THE SIKH COURT

THE author of *Gulabnama* says that Gulab Singh was taken into Ranjit Singh's service as commander of a regiment on a monthly salary of Rs.275. This is not unlikely. Cunningham,[1] and, following him, most English writers, assert that Gulab Singh was employed at the Lahore Court as a running footman. This is quite improbable. It is clear that he was personally well known to Ranjit Singh and was holding a sufficiently important post near the Maharajah, for we find him, almost immediately after his own appointment, presenting his brother Mian Dhyan Singh at Court. Dhyan Singh was appointed on a monthly salary of Rs.60. Kishore Singh was also introduced to Maharajah Ranjit Singh, who appointed him to a civil post carrying Rs.55 a month.

In 1809, when Gulab Singh joined the Lahore Court, Ranjit Singh had not attained that eminence which at a later time earned for him the sobriquet of the Lion of the Punjab. He was as yet looked upon only as a rising potentate. His empire, which later on extended from the Pamirs to Sind and from Peshawar to the Sutlej and included within it not

[1] J. D. Cunningham, *History of the Sikhs*, p. 190.

only the Punjab but the North-West Frontier provinces and the territories of Jammu and Kashmir, was then only in formation. Ranjit Singh had acquired Lahore and the title of Rajah only in 1799. It was not until 1802, when he was just twenty-two, that he attacked and conquered Amritsar. Moreover, the power of the Sikh misls had not been finally broken till the destruction of the Nakkai confederacy in 1810. In 1809, the English concluded a treaty with him, as they saw in him a formidable frontier chief who was likely to unite the forces of the Khalsa under his personal rule. The Maharajah was daily strengthening his position, but it is necessary to remember that in 1809, when Gulab Singh joined his service, he was not yet the renowned and masterful King of the Punjab, but merely an important and rising Sikh ruler, claiming his title from the grant of the Afghan and his power from the alliance of the Sikh misls.

In 1812 Ranjit Singh started on his first expedition against Kashmir, in alliance with Fateh Khan, Minister of Shah Mahmud of Kabul. To understand the events which follow it is necessary to realise the position of the Afghan kingdom at this time. In the beginning of the nineteenth century the Durrani Empire comprised the whole of the Indus Valley, including Multan, Kashmir, and the hilly provinces attached to the valley. Peshawar,

Attock, and other places were considered integral parts of Afghanistan in the same sense as are Herat and Kandahar to-day. Kashmir was a recognised province of the empire. Zaman Shah, whose name had once been a terror to the East India Company, was on the throne in 1803, and it was from him that Ranjit Singh had received the title of Rajah in 1799. But in that year the Shah was deposed by Mahmud, his brother. Mahmud was in turn expelled by Shah Shuja, the unlucky sovereign who plays an important part in the history of the Punjab during the next thirty years. In 1809 the Bakarzai tribe again rebelled, and its chief, Fateh Khan, son of Poynda Khan, put Mahmud back on the throne, keeping to himself all the power in the State as Wazir. It was this Wazir Fateh Khan who allied himself with Ranjit in the invasion of Kashmir. General Mokam Chand was, on behalf of Ranjit Singh, in charge of the expedition, and the army marched up the Jhelum Valley. The alliance, however, broke on the way, as Fateh Khan tried to forestall the Dewan. Though the trick failed, Fateh Khan stuck to Kashmir. In 1813 the Maharajah attempted to oust Fateh Khan, and Ranjit Singh led a force in person into Kashmir. In this campaign Gulab Singh's regiment played a prominent part. On the advice of Ajar Khan of Rajouri, the Punjab army was divided into two portions, one section proceeding by way of Poonch under Ranjit himself, and the other under Dewan Ram Dyal, the grandson of the great Mokam Chand, by way of Bahramagalla. This division of the invading forces was disastrous, and Ram Dyal's army was cut to pieces by the Governor of Kashmir. The people also rose in rebellion behind the Sikhs. Gulab Singh and his company escaped with difficulty. In these perilous circumstances Gulab Singh showed the greatest courage in reassembling his forces and bringing them back safely. His father, Mian Kishore Singh, was wounded in this campaign. Ranjit Singh was greatly pleased with Gulab Singh's achievement, and gave him as jagirs Kharoti and Beyol and promoted him in his command.

At this time Mian Mota, the brother of Zorawar Singh, was murdered at Jammu through the intrigue of the Sikh Governor, and this event had a great influence on the career of Gulab Singh. We have already mentioned how the ambitious Rani Bindral had tried to take in her own hands the management of Jammu. The great hindrance to her plans was her uncle-in-law, Mian Mota Singh, who wielded great influence in the area. In 1812 Prince Kharrak Singh, the eldest son of Ranjit Singh, to whom Jammu was allotted as jagir, came to take possession of the city, and the Rani Bindral insinuated herself into favour with him. When the matter came to the knowledge of Ranjit Singh he ordered that the government of Jammu should be carried on in consultation with Mota Singh, and that he should be given a jagir bringing an annual income of Rs.12,000. This displeased the Rani greatly. When Kharrak Singh returned to Lahore he left Dewan Ajit Singh, Khullal of Gujerat, as Governor. The Rani, nothing daunted, intrigued with the Dewan, over whom she acquired great influence, and persuaded him to order the assassination of Mian Mota. This dastardly act was entrusted to two bravos, Traho and Sutro, who waylaid the mian and murdered him (1812).

One day, on their way to the Durbar at Lahore, Gulab Singh and Dhyan Singh encountered the murderers by the Bhati Gate and killed them in broad daylight. This action of the brothers caused a great sensation in Lahore, especially as these bravos were known to be under the protection of Prince Kharrak Singh. When Gulab Singh arrived at the Durbar the guards insisted on his surrendering his arms, which he refused to do. But Ranjit Singh took no notice of the incident, merely remarking that Gulab Singh should be more careful of his life. As he feared vengeance against the brothers, Ranjit Singh took care to put Dhyan Singh under Jamadar Khushal Singh, the famous Deorhi Officer or Chamberlain, who was at the time the most powerful personage at the Lahore Court.

Gulab Singh continued to rise in favour at the Lahore Court. At the siege of Jullundur he distinguished himself greatly, and was as a reward given additional jagirs of Chohana and Ramgarh. He was also empowered to raise as his own a company of 200 soldiers. This was the first force which owned Gulab Singh as its master. Ramgarh was reduced after some fighting, and Mian Zorawar Singh, with the family, took his permanent abode there. (It was at this place that Rajah Hira Singh was born.)

In 1815 Reasi, which is an important district in the proximity of Jammu, was awarded by Ranjit Singh as jagir to Mian Dewan Singh. Dewan Singh was the mortal enemy of Gulab Singh, and was one of the prime movers in the murder of Mota Singh. The ambitious chief, who dreamed of uniting all the hilly country over which his ancestor ruled into one State, naturally disliked the grant of Reasi to his enemy. As Dewan Singh was in the plains, Gulab Singh forestalled him and took possession of the area and put Wazir Zorawar Kalhoria, who was destined to earn undying fame as the conqueror of Ladak and Tibet, in charge of its defence. But his rival was a person of courage and influence. Dewan Singh had a large body of supporters, and at their instigation the whole district rose against Gulab Singh's unauthorised action. Zorawar was hard pressed in the fort, but the courage, fortitude, and resourcefulness which later on enabled him to conquer Ladak and Baltistan and lead an army into the heart of Tibet were not to be shaken by a local siege. He held the town in spite of all that the enemy could do. When Kishore Singh heard of the plight of the garrison at Reasi he sent a few servants to Jammu to inform Gulab Singh of the position. Gulab Singh was away in Lahore, but Dewan Amir Chand, the father of Dewan Jwala Sahai, who figures greatly in the later events of Gulab Singh's life, was in charge of affairs at Jammu, and he took up the matter with all expedition. There was no money in the treasury and there were no troops at his command. He tried to enlist the support of the Rajputs of the locality, but they, envious of Gulab Singh's rising position, held back. Amir Chand, however, was not a man who easily lost hope. He borrowed money from a merchant in Jammu, collected as much arms and ammunition as he could, and marched on Reasi. He had only forty men with him, but the Dewan obtained recruits on the way by producing a letter which he declared he had received from Gulab Singh to the effect that he would soon be coming himself and that he was in greater favour than ever at Lahore. With his followers thus increased he reached Reasi and relieved the garrison.

Almost within six years of his taking service

in Lahore, Gulab Singh had become an important grandee. He was in possession of many estates granted to him as jagir in recognition of his meritorious services, and he was among the few noblemen entitled to maintain a regular force of their own. Rajah Dhyan Singh also had advanced greatly in the favour of the Lahore Durbar.

In all the campaigns that the Sikh King carried on at this time Gulab Singh played a prominent part. Especially at the siege of Multan, in 1819, his personal bravery attracted Ranjit Singh's favourable notice. During the siege, which was conducted under the supervision of Ranjit Singh, one of the Sikh sardars fell dead at the very foot of the fort. The besiegers were being subjected to heavy cannon fire, and Ranjit Singh, who was fond of the dead sardar, commanded his officers to ride to the spot and bring back the dead body. No one ventured except Gulab Singh, who, without a word, rushed forward to the amazement of the whole army and brought back on his horse the body of his dead comrade.

In the frontier campaigns of Ranjit Singh between 1815 and 1820 Gulab Singh played a prominent and noteworthy part. The most important among them was the campaign against the tribe of Yusuf in 1819 which enabled Ranjit Singh to acquire Peshawar.

In 1819 Dhyan Singh was made Deorhi Officer,

or Grand Chamberlain, when Khushal Singh was sent as Governor of Multan. This appointment gave Dhyan Singh great influence over the Maharajah.

At this time the hilly area behind Jammu was being terrorised by an intrepid chief by the name of Mian Dedo. His word was law in the interior, and he even attacked the Sikh garrison, which numbered over 2,000, in the Jammu fort.[1] The local Rajput chiefs sympathised with him and afforded no help to the Sikhs. The Sikhs laid hands on some of the leading Rajputs, held them as hostages, and sent them to Sheikhpura to be detained in prison. Dewan Bhavani Das called Juna Dingh, a Rajput chieftain, to Jammu and cut him to pieces on the mere suspicion of having given refuge to Dedo. This was the signal for a general revolt. The whole country behind the Jammu town threw off the Sikh yoke, and Mian Dedo placed himself at the head of the popular discontent. His adventures took a more serious turn, and it became clear either that he had to be put down or that Ranjit Singh would have to withdraw to Sialkot.

In open Durbar one day Gulab Singh requested to be entrusted with the duty of putting down this insurrection. Having secured the commission he

[1] Smyth, *History of the Reigning Family of Lahore*. (Calcutta, 1847.)

started without delay, accompanied by Sardar Attar Singh Kallol and Sardar Jagan Nath Singh, of Attari. At his request the Rajput chiefs held as hostages at Sheikhpura were released. On reaching Jammu he proceeded vigorously to put down the rebellion. The local chiefs surrendered, but Mian Dedo continued his depredations. The methods by which he brought Dedo to book were characteristic. It soon came to his notice that Dedo got free supplies in all the villages where he went. The bandit chief used to requisition all that he wanted, and the villagers out of fear obeyed him. It was necessary to stop this if Dedo was to be captured. Gulab Singh hit on a stratagem. He suddenly appeared in some out-of-the-way villages and demanded supplies in the name of Dedo. When the villagers brought the supplies he announced his identity, and punished them for helping the bandit. When this procedure was followed in a few villages Dedo found it difficult to get any supplies, because, when he sent his requisition, the villagers, not knowing whether it was Gulab Singh trying their loyalty or Dedo himself, refused to obey.

After this manœuvre Gulab Singh marched on Jugti, which was the headquarters of Dedo. The chief himself was not there, but his aged father defended the place, though he was past ninety. The old man was cut to pieces at the entrance to his house by Attar Singh Kallol. Dedo then took refuge on the Trikuti peak. The peak was surrounded, and in this last extremity Dedo, after committing his wife and children to the care of one Brahmachari, who was in the temple of the Devi, came out bravely to sell his life dear. He encountered Attar Singh, who was responsible for the death of his aged father, and challenged him to open combat. Attar Singh was killed in the fight, but Dedo was immediately shot dead by Gulab Singh's soldiers.

In 1820 Jammu was given to Gulab Singh in farm. Ranjit Singh followed the medieval system of farming out provinces for revenue. Jammu had always been considered an unruly and difficult province to manage, and when the government of the province was offered to Gulab Singh he represented that it was impossible to collect the revenue, as the place had not been completely subdued. Ranjit Singh therefore allowed him to keep an army of his own and gave him the title of Rajah, and Mian Kishore Singh and Dewan Chand were sent to instal him in his office. This appointment to the government of Jammu should not be confused with the conferment of that principality as an hereditary possession three years later.

In 1821 Gulab Singh undertook the conquest of Khistwar. With this object he marched into the interior. On the way he called on Dyal Chand,

Rajah of Chenani, to do him obeisance. But as the Rajah would not come, Gulab Singh sent a man to call on him. The Rajah agreed to help in the conquest of Khistwar. The Chenab was crossed and the camp was pitched at Doda. Instead of directly attacking Khistwar he decided first to create political dissension in the State. Rajah Tej Singh, of Khistwar, was a suspicious man, but he was served by an able Minister, by name Wazir Lakhpat. Gulab Singh sent a letter to Lakhpat in the following words: 'I have received your petition and understood the contents. You are ordered to present yourself before me without delay and to discharge the duties entrusted to you satisfactorily, in which case my kindness will always protect you.'

Gulab Singh had taken good care that the letter should fall into the hands of the Rajah and not the Wazir. Not suspecting the stratagem of Gulab Singh, the Rajah imprisoned the Wazir, who, however, escaped to Bhadarwah. Khistwar was conquered, and this was Gulab Singh's first independent province.

Wazir Lakhpat was taken into Gulab Singh's service, and till his death in Kashmir, in 1846, he was one of the Rajah's most trusted officers. He proved himself loyal to his master, and Gulab Singh sent him on many notable expeditions.

An important expedition entrusted to Gulab

Singh at this time was the reduction of Rajouri, which was under the rule of a local Mussulman dynasty of Rajput descent. The Rajah, whose name was Ajar Khan, had given Ranjit Singh more than one occasion for enmity. It was his double-faced advice which brought disaster on Ranjit Singh in his expedition against Kashmir in 1813. Gulab Singh was entrusted with the duty of capturing him, in which he succeeded.

These distinguished services to the Lahore Government were rewarded by the Maharajah with the grant to Gulab Singh and his successors of the principality of Jammu, with the hereditary title of Rajah. For this purpose the Maharajah moved in great state to Aknoor. The town of Aknoor is situated at the point where the Chenab debouches into the plain. Placed on the bank of the river, with a magnificent range of mountains as a background, the town presents a most striking appearance. The fort at Aknoor was built at the end of the eighteenth century by Mian Tej Singh, who was a feudatory of Rajah Ranjit Deo. Ranjit Singh took up his residence in the fort and made preparation for the ceremony of *Rajtilak*, or installation.

Gulab Singh, who was away on an expedition in the hills, was summoned to the royal presence. On 4th Ashad, 1879 (A.D. 1822), Ranjit Singh installed him on the Gadi and personally performed the *Raj-*

tilak. When marking the saffron on the forehead, Ranjit Singh, instead of marking it upwards, as is the custom, marked it downwards. When a courtier asked him why he had departed from established usage, Ranjit Singh replied: 'I firmly sowed the seed in the soil that it may thrive well, hold its root strong in the earth, and last for ever.' On the same day he gave to Mian Suchet Singh the jagir of Ramnagar with the title of Rajah. Gulab Singh was surprised that Dhyan Singh, who was then in high favour with the Maharajah, was not given any principality, and requested that, since both he and Suchet Singh had been so honoured, Dhyan Singh also might be granted a jagir. Ranjit Singh was highly pleased with this thoughtfulness on the part of Gulab Singh, and remarked that so far as Dhyan Singh was concerned, he did not propose to award him a jagir, as his intention was to make him a *Raja-i-Rajagan*, or a 'Rajah of Rajahs.'

A copy of the sanad that Maharajah Ranjit Singh granted to Gulab Singh is given below in translation:

> On this auspicious occasion, with extreme joy and with heartfelt love, I grant to Rajah Gulab Singh, in recognition of his conscientious and loyal service, the government of the Chakla of Jammu, which from time immemorial has been in the possession of his family. He and

his brothers, Dhyan Singh and Suchet Singh, appeared in my Court at a very early age and loyally and devotedly served me and the State. Their ancestors also served faithfully for a long time under my father Mahan Singh Ji of happy memory. They spared no pains to render their services to me promptly and submissively and to give me satisfaction. They have always been found faithful to me and loyal to the State. They have shed their blood freely in many campaigns such as the conquest of Kashmir, the reduction of Multan, the punishment of the rebels, the suppression of rebellion on the frontier and the fight with the forces of Kabul. In consideration of these and other services I grant the government of the Chakla of Jammu to Rajah Gulab Singh and his descendants, and I myself mark the forehead of this loyal and devoted servant of mine with the emblem of sovereignty. With great pleasure I also grant Rajah Suchet Singh the government of Ramnagar to be his own and his descendants' as a reward for the great services he has rendered to me. He and his descendants may dispose of its income on their own account provided that the Rajahs be as loyal to the State henceforward as they have been till now, that they receive our descendants with no less honour and submission and that their descendants be as loyal to us and our descendants. In witness of this I grant this Purwana of mine with my own hands together with a bunch of saffron.

Dated 4th Ashad, 1879 (Vikram).

Gulab Singh was just thirty years old. He had every reason to be proud of his achievements. With nothing but a name, a proud ancestry, and his own talents he had succeeded in getting back his hereditary possession and in being recognised by Ranjit Singh as the Rajah of Jammu. His fame as a warrior had reverberated through the Punjab. He had become an important grandee at the Lahore Court, where his brothers also stood high in favour. Dhyan Singh, though hardly more than twenty-seven, was, next to Aziz-ud-Din and Dina Nath, the most influential man in the Lahore Government. He held, besides, the post of Deorhi Officer, which kept him in intimate touch with Ranjit Singh. Suchet Singh was reputed to be the most handsome man in the Sikh army, and he was also equally in favour with the Maharajah.

After the conferment of Jammu, Gulab Singh was sent on an expedition against Azam Khan, of Tihri, on the frontier. The army was nominally under the command of Prince Sher Singh, but to him were attached Gulab Singh and Hari Singh Nalwa. The latter was the noblest and the most gallant of the Sikh generals of his time, the very embodiment of honour, chivalry, and courage. His position at the Court was high, and he was the idol of the Sikhs. With these two commanders attached to him Sher Singh marched to the frontier. A moulvi by the name of Khalifa Saidulla had roused the religious fanaticism of the tribes, and the campaign was more difficult than was originally anticipated. Immediate victory did not fall to the Sikh army, and the handsome but chicken-hearted Sher Singh proposed to retire. He was, however, dissuaded from this disastrous course by Gulab Singh, whose brothers had also by this time joined the campaign.

In 1823 Dost Mohammad, brother of Wazir Fateh Khan, became King of Kabul. The kingdom which he inherited had already lost Multan, Kashmir, Peshawar, Dera Ghazi Khan, and Dera Ismail Khan. The frontier was naturally the scene of further disturbance, and in 1826 Saidulla again raised the standard of revolt.

Sardar Budha Singh, who was in charge of the frontier districts, was sorely tried, and Gulab Singh, who was in Jammu, received orders to go to his help. The Rajah immediately sent his forces under Dewan Amir Chand, and himself joined them later, by forced marches, at Peshawar. Hari Singh Nalwa also joined him there. The Pathans, on retreating, had destroyed the bridge at Attock, which made further advance difficult. Leaving the army behind, Gulab Singh crossed the Indus with a very small force and attacked the enemy from behind a hill with only 300 men. While the fray was in progress Hari Singh Nalwa, who was not to be left behind in any act of valour, joined him. The enemy, not knowing the strength of the attacking force, retired. Gulab Singh was wounded in the arm on this occasion. For fifteen days the army halted there. The Sikh chief proposed the erection of entrenchments with a view to defending the position, but Gulab Singh, with superior wisdom, pointed out that in view of the strength of the enemy safety lay for the Sikhs in their mobility, and dissuaded Hari Singh from the course which he had suggested. The tribes sought the help of Dost Mohammad, who marched towards the Indus with a large force. Ranjit Singh, who realised the gravity of the danger, himself arrived at the scene of the operations with the leading nobles in his train. Before any fighting took place, Dost Mohammad's discontented brothers, Pir Mohammad and Sultan Mohammad, put themselves in touch with Gulab Singh. Sultan Mohammad requested a personal interview with Gulab Singh with the object of negotiating for his own safety. An interview was arranged between him and Ranjit Singh, who was well pleased at the collapse of the Afghan invasion. The Sikh ruler accepted the submission of Sultan Mohammad,[1] and agreed to invest him with Peshawar. This proposal made Hari Singh angry, and it was only at the personal intervention of Gulab Singh that Sultan Mohammad was not sent back to his brother. Furious at the desertion of his own brothers, Dost Mohammad marched back to Kabul.

In 1825 Gulab Singh made further conquests in the hilly tracts lying in the interior of Jammu. With Dewan Amir Chand and Mian Gulab Singh Dhulpatia he took the fort of Samarth and reduced the surrounding country. In the period between 1820 and 1827 Gulab Singh brought under his effective control the numerous principalities lying between the Kashmir Valley and Jammu, except Poonch, which was the jagir of Dhyan Singh; Jasrota, which was given to Hira Singh, and Ramnagar, which belonged to Suchet Singh. Gulab Singh himself conquered Reasi, Khistwar, Rajouri, and Samarth, which, with Jammu, formed a very extensive dominion for a subordinate prince.

To the management of his principality Gulab

[1] Sultan Mohammad became one of the leading sardars at the Lahore Court, and was esteemed by all parties as a nobleman of great courage.

Singh devoted great attention. Other chiefs of the Lahore Court who held jagirs spent most of their time in Lahore in attendance on Ranjit Singh, and depended on their managers for their income—a system that led to great abuses. The managers, not being under the control of their masters, were only concerned to squeeze out of the cultivators as much money as they could, and took no interest in their welfare. The chiefs were only interested in getting money regularly and the managers only in satisfying their masters and in enriching themselves. Gulab Singh, from the time that Jammu was conferred on him, followed a totally different policy. He stayed mostly in Jammu and appeared at Lahore only when summoned. He took great personal interest in the management of his property and the government of his dominions which, by their hilly nature and by the independent character of their people, called for personal attention.

In this duty he was helped by a family of remarkable men, whose devotion to him and whose ability in his service he rewarded most munificently. This was the family of which Dewan Jwala Sahai, later the Prime Minister of the State and Gulab Singh's plenipotentiary in the negotiation of all confidential matters, was the most important member. Dewan Amir Chand, the father of Jwala Sahai, was the managing agent of Gulab Singh in the Newal Ilaqa, and when Jammu was granted as an hereditary principality in 1823, Amir Chand was made Madar-ul-Maham, or Chief Minister, of Jammu. In 1836, when Dewan Amir Chand died, his eldest son, Dewan Jwala Sahai, became the chief adviser and Dewan of Gulab Singh. Jwala Sahai had two brothers, Dewan Hari Chand and Dewan Nihal Chand, both of whom were employed by Gulab Singh in important civil and military capacities.

The attention which Gulab Singh devoted to the management of his fiefs and the good results that followed from it attracted the attention of Ranjit Singh. The ruler of the Punjab, who was quick to realise the value of such government, entrusted Gulab Singh with the management of the following areas at different times to be held as farms from the Lahore Durbar:

Behra, Miani, Fadka, and the salt mines of Pinddadan Khan.

Farms:	*Estimated Income.*
	Rs.
Chukh Huzara and Pukhlee Dhumtour	150,000
Djunnee, Kuttas, and Chakkowall	100,000
Sialkot	50,000
Salt mines	about 8 lakhs

He was also given the following jagirs:

Bhadarwah (part), Padar, Jammu, Chenai, Reasi, Khistwar, Aknoor, Rajouri.

The following jagirs were held by the other members of the family:

	Estimated Income.
Suchet Singh:	Rs.
Besholi	75,000
Jasrota	125,000
Makkot, Bhuddo, and Bhadralta	

Dhyan Singh:

Samba, Bhimber, Poonch, Kottlee.

Town duties at Amritsar and Lahore.

Gulab Singh was able to follow this policy of staying on his estate and looking after its management only because he knew that his interest and the interests of his family were safe at Lahore. When the government is personal and is dependent on the whims of a ruler, a courtier, however able and useful, is likely to be forgotten unless he is present at Court and is in a position to compete for the favour of the sovereign. Fortunately, Gulab Singh had not to do this. The presence of his brother, Dhyan Singh, at Court as Lord Chamberlain and later as Prime Minister, and the favour to which Hira Singh, Dhyan Singh's son, attained, were sufficient guarantee for him. In fact, all the three brothers consciously followed as a policy the celebrated saying of a French Marshal: 'He who hurts my brother hurts me.' The political influence of Dhyan Singh left Gulab Singh free to look after the affairs of his territories, to raise and keep intact a reserve of money, and to train and equip an army. He was left free to consolidate his authority and to perfect a military machine with which to conquer new countries when occasion arose. He was shrewd enough to foresee that all these precautions would be required once the strong hand of Ranjit Singh was removed from the Punjab.

By 1835 Gulab Singh had become the most important feudatory of Ranjit Singh and the most powerful personality at the Lahore Court. Besides his own principality he held in farm some of the most productive lands in the Punjab. His army, which was under renowned commanders, had already attacked Ladak. Ranjit Singh, who never doubted Gulab Singh's loyalty, was in no way envious of the overgrown power of his dependent and continued to show favour to him and his family.

CHAPTER III

GULAB SINGH AND THE SIKH ANARCHY

On the 27th June, 1839, Maharajah Ranjit Singh died at the age of 59. A few months before his death his powers had visibly declined and the government of the kingdom was in the hands of Dhyan Singh, the Dewan. Rajah Dina Nath had the control of finances, and Fakir Aziz-ud-Din was the Foreign Minister, but the authority of the State was in the hands of Rajah Dhyan Singh. Ranjit Singh was succeeded by his son, Kharrak Singh, an imbecile and a voluptuary, who was in the hands of his favourite, Chet Singh. This alienated the great officers of the Court, who were not willing to surrender their power to a Court favourite. Forgetting their own quarrels, the leading rajahs and sardars joined hands, and on 8th October, 1839, the most important of them, with Nao Nihal Singh, the heir apparent, at their head, forced their way into the palace. Kharrak Singh was tying his turban. Gulab Singh killed the doorkeeper and broke open the door, though Kharrak Singh tried to lock it from inside. The Maharajah refused to yield up his favourite and held him in his arms, but Gulab Singh tore him away. Chet Singh ran into a dungeon, where Dhyan Singh followed him and killed him.

After this, Gulab Singh left the Lahore Court and went on a pilgrimage to Gaya, returning thence direct to Jammu. The death of Chet Singh had, however, not improved the prospects of his family. Nao Nihal Singh, Kharrak Singh's young son, was an able and ambitious prince, and it was his undisguised object to work the ruin of Gulab Singh and his brothers. He decided to attack Jammu and reduce the too presumptuous subject, who by this time held Jammu, Reasi, Khistwar, Rajouri, and other hill principalities, besides numerous districts given on contract by the Lahore Government. To reduce him was not an easy affair. Nao Nihal Singh realised this and proceeded systematically to concentrate a very strong force at favourable points. On the pretext of preparing for a campaign against Mandi, a large force under General Ventura was concentrated to the east of Jammu. Nao Nihal Singh was compelled, however, to postpone the campaign for a few months owing to Afghan troubles. When these were over, and before he could undertake the campaign, Kharrak Singh died on the 5th November, 1840. But the same day Nao Nihal Singh also died as a result of an accidental fall of an archway under which he passed on his return from the obsequies of his father. Gulab Singh's eldest son, Ootam (Randhir) Singh, rode with the prince and died as a result of the same accident. According to Dr. Honigberger,[1] who was present at Lahore and treated the Prince, Dhyan Singh himself was injured. These facts should dispose of the baseless suggestion of Cunningham[2] that the fall of the archway was not accidental, but was the result of design by the Jammu rajahs.

The death of Nao Nihal Singh left the Lahore throne vacant. Dhyan Singh favoured Sher Singh, a reputed son of Ranjit Singh, but Gulab Singh, Khushal Singh, and Bhai Ram Singh declared themselves in favour of Chand Kour, the widow of Kharrak Singh, who assumed the reins of government with the title of Regent. A compromise was for the time arranged, and Sher Singh accepted the position of Vice-Regent. Dhyan Singh kept aloof from this arrangement and returned to Jammu. From there he negotiated with Sher Singh, who also had withdrawn from the capital. Winning over some divisions of the army, Sher Singh declared himself King and attacked Lahore, where he had been promised support by Dhyan Singh. But the Prime Minister was away in Jammu, and Gulab Singh, who was in the fort, refused to surrender it. Sher Singh had, in fact, calculated without the host. Gulab Singh's loyalty to Mai Chand Kour upset all

[1] Dr. Honigberger, *Thirty-five Years in the East,* p. 103. (London, 1852.)

[2] *History of the Sikhs,* p. 244.

his plans. Sher Singh, who marched on the capital with a large force, was held up in front of Lahore. Gulab Singh advised Mai Sahib to offer resistance, and himself took command of the forces within the citadel. With him in the fort were Rajah Hira Singh, Attar Singh Sindhanwalla, and Mansul Singh Sindu. The city was put in a state of defence and guns were placed at all the city gates. Gulab Singh was indefatigable in his efforts to strengthen the defence, and gave four months' pay as gratuity to the garrison. He personally went round to every post, inspected the garrison, and encouraged them by promises and rewards. This unexpected decision to hold the fort against the army which had gone over to Sher Singh created a difficult situation for that Prince. Sher Singh was now forced to lay siege[1] to Lahore and to declare war against the constituted authority of the State, while Gulab Singh stood forward as the champion of the Sikh Government. Sher Singh, however, found unexpected support in Rajah Suchet Singh and General Ventura, both of whom acknowledged him as King. He had now under his command 70,000 troops. By bribing the gatekeeper, Sher Singh was able to gain access to the city, but Gulab Singh defended the

[1] This famous siege is described in many histories. The description given by Smyth, *Reigning Family of Lahore*, pp. 43-61, is the most detailed.

citadel with heroism in the face of vastly superior numbers. The attack began against the Hazuri Bagh Gate. The gate was blown in, but the small force which entered the city was shot down by the Dogra soldiers of Gulab Singh placed behind the gate, and the attack was repulsed. Soon afterwards Sher Singh was forced to withdraw from Hazuri Bagh. Successive assaults were repulsed and Gulab Singh maintained himself in the fort for five days. At the end of the fifth day news arrived that Dhyan Singh was approaching Lahore. He was given a royal ovation by the populace and Sher Singh personally went to receive him at the city gate.

By this time Chand Kour was in a state of great fear, and she was anxious that peace should be restored on the condition of proper provision for herself. She accordingly wrote the following letter to Gulab Singh:

To the wise and enlightened Rajah Gulab Singh, Chief Minister of the State.

> This imperial Irshad is issued to you now. I thank you very much and Rajah Hira Singh Bahadur, Sardar Mangal Singh, Sardar Sultan Mohamad Khan, and other faithful nobles who helped you in the siege, for the devotion, loyalty and obedience which you displayed so heroically in holding your own against the

> usurper. For this I again thank you sincerely. You proved yourself most faithful to the Sircar and the Sircar's obligations to you are very great. You are now at liberty to put an end to the fight in any manner you choose. The Sircar leaves the matter to your discretion. The only thing the Sircar wants is that you should settle the matter as quickly as possible. Settle the matter very soon and receive the Sircar's kindness.

On this Gulab Singh opened negotiations. He made the following three conditions: (1) The Mai Sahib should be honoured and given a suitable position, (2) all the sardars on her side should be pardoned, and (3) Gulab Singh and other leading nobles should be taken into favour.

Sher Singh accepted all these conditions and sent to Gulab Singh the following message, signed by himself and all the leading nobles on his side:

To the wise and enlightened Rajah Gulab Singh, Minister of State.

> This imperial Irshad is issued to you now. Please stop firing the guns in the fort. Bhai Uttam Singh and Babu Blahyam Singh are appointed by the Sircar to come to you to the presence, and if you attend you will be treated

> with honour and titles. You can rest assured of it. We are very kindly disposed towards you. If you yourself do not like to come, kindly ask Mai Saheb to come out of the fort for Sri Granth Sahib's sake. She will be safe and welcome. Whoever prefers to die in the fort, keep him there, but come yourself. Your three conditions will be fulfilled if you come. Leave all anxieties aside and rest assured of our kindness and help.

On a truce being arranged, Sher Singh sent a message praising the services which Gulab Singh and his brothers had rendered and promising to abide by the advice of the chiefs. His conditions were agreed to, the fort was surrendered, and Gulab Singh marched out at midnight on the 19th January, 1841.

Although Gulab Singh was offered the position of minister under the new regime, he was in no mood to take part in the intrigues of Lahore, and preferred to return to his own dominions. It is said that when he left the fort he carried away with him the accumulated treasures of Ranjit Singh which were there. Sixteen carts were filled with rupees and other silver coins, while 500 horsemen were each entrusted with a bag of gold mohurs. With this vast treasure he returned to Jammu, where his presence was urgently required in support of the Ladak campaign, which was now in full swing.[1]

In 1841 disaster overtook the British arms in Afghanistan. The garrison at Jalalabad was being besieged, and to relieve it a British force was equipped at Peshawar. The co-operation of the Sikhs was necessary. To obtain this, Major (later Sir Henry) Lawrence was sent to Peshawar. His duty was to keep the Sikhs in good humour and to secure from them as much help as possible. To co-operate with the British expedition which was being organised on the frontier, the Lahore Government very reluctantly deputed Gulab Singh, who was at that time at Hazara. Gulab Singh's position was by no means easy. He knew well enough that the Lahore authorities were not in any way anxious to help the British in their Kabul expedition. At the same time, being gifted with farsighted views in politics, he knew that this was the occasion to secure the firm friendship of the British. He was therefore personally anxious to afford all help, provided it was clearly understood that the obligation was to him and not to the Lahore Government. The position of the British was desperate. They had been driven out of Afghanistan. Their own base was far away, and on their line of communication was the Sikh State, whose neutrality, if not help, was essential

[1] See *infra*.

for success. The Lahore Government was reluctant to afford any help, and this was known to the British authorities. Gulab Singh realised the full strength of his position—namely, that if effective help could be rendered to the British through his influence and authority, then their friendship towards him would be assured.

Before Gulab Singh arrived on the scene all hope of co-operation with the Sikhs had come to an end. On the 19th January, 1842, the British force was beaten back at the Khyber Pass. As the British entered Khyber the Sikhs quietly marched back to Peshawar.[1] The Nuseeb battalions consisting of Mussulmans had mutinied at the suggestion of co-operation with the British against Afghanistan. They threatened to attack the retreating force in the rear. It was then that General Pollock was chosen for the command of the army, and he marched through the Punjab territory to the rendezvous at Peshawar. Gulab Singh, who knew when not to hurry, also arrived in Peshawar, and struck his tents on the left bank of the river. His orders were 'to march to Peshawar, to coerce all mutineers, and co-operate with the English.' The Rajah, however, encamped on the left side of the river, and the first communication he addressed to Major Lawrence

[1] Edwardes and Merivale, *Life of Sir Henry Lawrence*, Third Edition, p. 223.

was a mild hint not to proceed by the direct road from Peshawar to Attock as he might be attacked by the Nuseeb battalions.[1] This advice was taken. Gulab Singh, however, managed to put the Nuseeb out of the way, and on the 3rd February, 1842, he moved on towards Peshawar in advance of the British troops. The Rajah took fully ten days from the Indus to Peshawar, a distance which he had on many former occasions covered in three days.

The original intention of the British Government was to persuade the Lahore Government to send a Sikh contingent with them to Jalalabad. Previous to the arrival of Gulab Singh the command of the frontier force was entrusted to General Mehtab Singh, whose attitude towards the British was frankly hostile.[2] When Gulab Singh arrived on the scene he told Lawrence that it was not advisable to take the Sikhs to Jalalabad. In their impatience the British commanders urged on the Rajah the necessity of making an example and of disbanding the battalions which had mutinied. Gulab Singh replied that the Sikhs had already borne him ill-will enough, and that he would not be supported in measures of coercion. In this there was some truth.[3] He naturally asked the British

[1] Edwardes and Merivale, *Life of Sir Henry Lawrence*, Third Edition, p. 223.

[2] *Ibid*., p. 225.

[3] *Ibid*.

Chief to allow him to proceed in his own manner. To this Lawrence agreed and Gulab Singh set out quietly to undermine the opposition of the Sikhs. Knowing the spirit and temper of the Sikh soldiers, he had no difficulty in dissuading them from active hostilities against the British army in Peshawar. If the Sikhs had turned against the British at that time the whole expedition would have ended disastrously. He pointed out to the Sikh soldiers that it was wiser to lead the British to the Khyber Pass and safely across it: that if they were defeated by the Afghans the property they left at Peshawar would belong to the Sikhs, while if they defeated the enemy the Sikhs could claim that it was through their help that the victory was won.

The Chiefs of the Khalsa army appreciated this wisdom. Gulab Singh was thus free to help the British with provisions and advice, and also to send some of his own troops with the British army. At this time news reached him of the débacle that had overtaken Zorawar in Central Tibet. He was naturally much grieved at this loss and sent Dewan Jwala Sahai on the 17th February, 1842, to Lawrence's camp with the request that the news of the disaster should not be made public, as it might cause a mutiny among his own troops. On the 20th February Gulab Singh paid a formal visit to General Pollock. The British commanders were getting tired of the dilatory tactics of Lahore and were determined to use the opportunity to come to some explanation. They received Gulab Singh with full military honours, and after all were seated Captain Makeson, an officer of 'commanding countenance and stately form uniting the beau ideal of the soldier and the diplomatist,' 'advanced through all the preliminaries of courtesy and the exigencies of the situation to the inevitable climax'[1] —asking for what purpose had the Sikh army been sent to Peshawar and what orders had been received from Lahore.

Gulab Singh was taken by surprise, but he was too experienced a diplomat to show it. His reply is thus described by the biographers of Lawrence:

> Those whose lot it has been to parley with that Ulysses of the Hills can call up before them the sweet deference of attention, the guileless benevolence, the childlike simplicity, and the masterly prolixity of fiction, parenthesis and anecdote with which Rajah Gulab Singh stroked his silver beard while listening to the question and then charmingly consumed the hours in avoiding a reply. Much had he to say about the past, the loyalty of his brothers and himself to the empire of their great master

[1] *Life of Sir Henry Lawrence*, Third Edition, p. 227.

> Ranjit Singh, and the wickedness of those who attributed to them schemes of an independent sovereignty. . . . But as to the future and what had now to be done to save the English garrisons still in Afganistan, Rajah Gulab Singh in all his flow of talk and illustration got no further than to remind the English that Dost Mohammad was a prisoner. But on being further questioned as to what were the orders of the Lahore Government, the Rajah produced a purwana in which he was ordered to consult General Pollock as to the objects the British Government had in view, what they proposed to effect and by what means, and to act in support of the British troops agreeably to the terms of this treaty.[1]

With this the Durbar terminated.

The British authorities began to think that something could not be had for nothing, and that unless Gulab Singh received an adequate *quid pro quo,* no help would be forthcoming. Lawrence had already suggested that a consideration should be offered to him. 'In plain terms, he explained, the troops should be paid extra *batta,* the Rajahs secured in their territory even with additions.' He added that 'if Gulab Singh assists the British efficiently

[1] *Life of Sir Henry Lawrence,* Third Edition, p. 227.

they should assist him to get possession of the Valley of Jalalabad, and endeavour to make some arrangement to secure it and Peshawar to his family.'[1]

These inducements he did not want. He had his own reasons for rendering whatever help lay in his power. More, he secured the neutrality of the Sikh regiments which at one time were actively hostile to the British. General Pollock was therefore enabled to enter the Khyber Pass on the 5th April, 1842.

The British Government sent an appreciative Kharita, dated 8th April, 1842, to Gulab Singh, through Mr. Clerk, their agent at Lahore, in which they said that they wrote to him with the pen of love and appreciation. 'We heard from the Chiefs of our army how wisely you planned for the help of our troops and how kindly you rendered this to them. . . . The fruit of the long-sown seed of friendship between us which was concealed for a long time has now come to light . . . you who are the flower of the garden of this world . . . the most delicious fruit of the tree of hope, we remember your troubles and difficulties in rendering help to our army: we shall never forget that.'

The basis of friendship between Henry Lawrence and Gulab Singh was thus well and truly laid.

[1] Letter to Clerk, 30th January, 1842.

The offer of Jalalabad was renewed, but a condition was made by Lord Ellenborough, the Governor-General, that Gulab Singh should give up Ladak and take the Afghan province in its stead. Gulab Singh was too shrewd a man not to see through this proposal. Ladak was in the vicinity of his own territories and could not be attacked either by the British or by the Sikhs. He was thus the uncontrolled master of that area which, though barren, was his own by right of conquest. Jalalabad, on the other hand, was far away from his base and could not be held against an enemy. Naturally, he refused the offer and was content with the friendship of the British.

The Lahore Government again fell into anarchy. Mai Chand Kour died in 1842. Relieved of the fear of usurpation, Sher Singh began to chafe against the authority of Dhyan Singh and sent for the Sindhanwalla sardars, Ajit Singh and Lehna Singh, to Lahore. Sher Singh had no love for the Sindhanwalla chiefs, but he hoped that their influence with the Sikhs would be an effective counterpoise to the influence of Dhyan Singh. But Sher Singh was not the man to follow a consistent policy. He soon alienated his best friends. Lehna Singh was imprisoned, Khushal Singh was not in favour at Court, the Jammu rajahs were greatly in disfavour. The idea that Sher Singh developed was to get hold of Gulab Singh and his brothers and kill all of them at one stroke. So in 1843 Gulab Singh was summoned to Kangra, where Sher Singh was camping at the time. Though he knew the object, Gulab Singh did not hesitate. Dhyan Singh, on the other hand, sent Hira Singh to Jasrota and went alone. Suchet Singh remained at Lahore. Failing to get all the brothers together, Sher Singh hesitated to act, treated Gulab Singh well and sent him back to Jammu.

In 1843 the marriage of Ranbir Singh to the daughter of Rajah Bijai Singh of Seeba was celebrated with great pomp. Ranbir Singh was the third and youngest, and the only surviving, son of Gulab Singh. Gulab Singh married early in life in 1809 a lady from the Rukwal Rajputs. By this lady he had three sons, Randhir Singh, Sohan Singh, and Ranbir Singh. Randhir Singh, as has been said above, died in company with Nao Nihal Singh as the result of an accident. Sohan Singh died young.

Ranbir Singh, born in 1829 at Ramgarh, was at this time only fourteen years old. As a young boy he was adopted by Rajah Suchet Singh, who had no son of his own. He spent his boyhood mostly at Ramnagar, which was the jagir of Suchet Singh.[1]

[1] Thakur Kashari Singh Bilawani, *Life of Ranbir Singh* in Urdu. (Jammu, 1890.)

The whole family gathered at Jammu—alas! for the last time. Rajah Dyhan Singh, the wise statesman and the leading Minister of the Sikh kingdom; Rajah Hira Singh, the accomplished courtier and the favourite of Ranjit Singh; Rajah Suchet Singh, reputed to be the most handsome man in the Sikh army, and the numerous dependents of each, all came together on the auspicious occasion. Gulab Singh could well claim that he had laid the foundation of the greatness of each one of them—all great and powerful men in the world now. He, the eldest, had spurned the life of the capital, and devoted himself entirely to the welfare of the family. He had raised armies, conquered kingdoms, and laid the foundation of a future greatness for his family such as few could claim. The occasion was really one for thanksgiving.

As soon as the marriage was over a messenger came from Lahore summoning Dhyan Singh. Against the advice of his brother he went. On his arrival he was received graciously by Sher Singh, but orders had already been issued to have him murdered. Dhyan Singh was advised of this by Sardar Ajit Singh Sindhanwalla. The sardars of Sindhanwalla played a double game in this matter. They hated Sher Singh and planned the fall of the Sovereign and Minister at one stroke. For this purpose they pursuaded the Maharajah that Dhyan

Singh had determined to destroy him and his safety lay in having the Minister assassinated first. Sher Singh believed it and authorised the Sindhanwalla chiefs in writing to get rid of Dhyan Singh. Having plotted Dhyan Singh's destruction, Ajit Singh went straight to him and informed him of the conspiracy and advised him to strike the blow first. Ajit Singh, who was reported to be a bosom friend of Sher Singh, was himself conspiring to get rid of Sher Singh. The next day at the review of troops Ajit Singh shot his Sovereign dead. Lehna Singh killed the boy Pratab Singh, the son of Sher Singh, at his devotions. After this dastardly action Ajit Singh mounted his horse and galloped towards Lahore with 300 followers.

Dhyan Singh, who was ignorant of the murder, was driving out at what is now the Badami Bagh when he was met by Ajit Singh and taken to the fort. As they ascended the fort, Ajit Singh, whom the Rajah, who had guessed the details of the tragedy, accused of treason, shot him dead (15th September, 1843).

Thus died Rajah Dhyan Singh, for over fifteen years Prime Minister of the Sikh State. As a statesman he had worked hard and successfully for the maintenance of the independence of the Punjab. He had resisted with all the means in his power the encroachment of the English Agent at Lahore on Sikh authority.[1] On one notable occasion he did not even hesitate to advise Sher Singh against a public interview with the Viceroy.[2] Polished and courtly, his personality was such as would have made a mark even in the Court of Shah Jehan or Louis XIV. Of his personal appearance, the following description is given by W. G. Osborne, Military Secretary to Lord Auckland : 'Rajah Dheean Singh is a noble specimen of the human race; rather above the usual height of the natives, with quick and intelligent eyes, high handsome forehead, and aquiline features; dressed in a magnificent helmet and cuirass of polished steel, a present from King Louis Philippe of France, he looked a model of manly beauty and intelligence."[3]

As soon as Dhyan Singh's death was known the partisans of the Jammu rajahs prepared for war. Hira Singh and Suchet Singh, who were in Lahore, immediately sent round word, and the whole aspect of Lahore changed. It became a city of rival camps. Rajah Hira Singh displayed unexpected calmness of mind on this occasion. He ascended the terrace of General Avitabile's house, and, having seated himself there, sent messages to the several sardars, requesting their immediate attendance. The call was

[1] Osborne, *Court and Camp of Ranjit Singh,* p. 75. (London, 1840.)

[2] J. D. Cunningham, *History of the Sikhs,* p. 267.

[3] Osborne, p. 74.

promptly obeyed and the sardars, with their troops, assembled at the foot of Budhuka Awa. Placing himself in front and unsheathing his sword, the young Rajah said: 'You know the traitors have killed our Sovereign, his innocent son, and my brave father, who loved you as much as he loved me. We are deprived of our Sovereign and I am fatherless. I now trust your courage, your patriotism, and your loyalty to our lamented King. Either uphold me firmly or kill me with this sword, as it is better to die with honour than to live in disgrace in the midst of enemies.'[1]

The response to this touching speech was immediate. The whole army agreed to follow him. Placing himself at the head of 40,000 troops, Hira Singh marched against the Sindhanwalla chiefs. Suchet Singh joined him in assaulting the fort, which fell into their hands. Ajit Singh met the fate of the murderer, and Lehna Singh also fell in the fight. The head of Ajit Singh was laid at the feet of the widowed rani of Dhyan Singh who, well content, declared: 'I am now fully satisfied.' Then she addressed Hira Singh and said: 'I will tell your father that you have acted the part of a brave and dutiful son.' After this she placed her dead husband's kulgee on Hira Singh's head and calmly ascended the pyre as sati.

[1] Syed Latif, *History of the Punjab*, p. 516.

After this, Suchet Singh and Hira Singh put Dhuleep Singh on the throne, and Hira Singh became Prime Minister. After the situation had settled down Gulab Singh, who had kept himself out of the intrigues of Lahore, came down from Jammu. He was requested by all to take up the post of Prime Minister. Especially was he pressed by Aziz-ud-Din, the Foreign Minister, who knew that a strong hand would be required to restore order and steer the ship of State through safe channels. But Gulab Singh, who knew the conditions at Lahore, refused to be inveigled into the whirlpool of Sikh politics, and returned to Jammu, taking Suchet Singh with him. He, however, left a body of his troops at Shahdara under Dewan Hari Chand, knowing well that Hira Singh might soon require help.

CHAPTER IV

GULAB SINGH AND THE SIKH ANARCHY *continued*

Hira Singh had great difficulties to face as Prime Minister. The claims of the boy Dhuleep Singh, who was proclaimed Maharajah, were contested by Peshwara Singh, a reputed son of Ranjit Singh. Rajah Suchet Singh, who was jealous of the power of Hira Singh, declared himself in favour of Peshwara Singh and Kashmira Singh, both reputed sons of Ranjit Singh, who refused to acknowledge Dhuleep Singh as King. Kashmira Singh, who held Sialkot as jagir, continued in his rebellious attitude, and Gulab Singh was ordered to subdue him. The Sikh soldiers would not fight against Kashmira Singh, as he was a son of the great Ranjit Singh; but Gulab Singh, with the help of his Dogra forces, captured the city, though he allowed the Princes to escape.

Suchet Singh had promised support to the rebellion, and the relations between uncle and nephew became strained. In March, 1844, Suchet Singh, who knew that the army was discontented, suddenly made his appearance in Lahore and tried to raise a rebellion. But his efforts did not succeed. Hira Singh acted with vigour. Suchet Singh had left his forces at Shahdara and had crossed the Ravi with only 400 men. But when he came to Lahore the regiments which had invited him refused to rise, and the next day Hira Singh surrounded his camp and he was overcome. He died fighting.

So far everything had gone well. Successful against Suchet Singh and others, Hira Singh tried to place himself in opposition to Gulab Singh. The immediate occasion was the claim to the property of Suchet Singh, which Gulab Singh had taken possession of on the latter's death. To proceed against Gulab Singh required some courage, but Hira Singh, whatever his other faults, did not lack that quality. Besides, he could claim that the properties of Suchet Singh were forfeit to Lahore owing to his rebellion. .Gulab Singh in taking possession of them had proceeded on the ground that Suchet Singh, who was childless, had adopted Ranbir Singh when the latter was still a child, and that therefore the dead Rajah's property was vested in him by right. Hira Singh also claimed that he was the legal heir. On Gulab Singh's refusal to yield, Hira Singh ordered that the towns and grants held by Gulab Singh in the Punjab on contract be forfeited, and he decided, further, to attack Jammu itself. Gulab Singh was prepared for this. But as a quarrel was likely to cause weakness to both, he agreed to give half of Suchet Singh's property to Hira Singh, and thereupon the towns and villages which had been taken away from him were restored.

Hira Singh could legitimately claim that within a short time he had restored order, suppressed all rebellions, and had the authority of Lahore recognised even by Gulab Singh. But his star was on the wane. The dissolute Rani Jindan and her lover, Lal Singh, turned to Jawahar Singh, the brother of the Rani, who was a man of some capacity, for help against the power of Hira Singh. Jawahar Singh took the boy Maharajah to the army and asked them to get rid of Hira Singh in order to make Dhuleep their real Sovereign. The army demurred to this, as Hira Singh was popular with them, but agreed to request him to surrender Julla, his favourite. Refusing to surrender his friend and realising the danger that surrounded him, Hira Singh left Lahore on his famous horse, Burchi Bahadur. But on the way the party was overtaken. Hira Singh died, fighting to the last, on 21st December, 1844.

The Lahore Durbar was not yet satisfied. Dhyan Singh, Suchet Singh, and Hira Singh were dead, but the oldest and most powerful of the Jammu family was still alive and well entrenched in his possessions. To get him into their power was not so easy. A pretext for a quarrel was soon found.

Hira Singh's property was declared confiscated. Rani Jindan sent Lala Rattan Chand and Baba Mian Singh to Gulab Singh with the demand that the possessions of Rajah Hira Singh should be surrended to Lahore and that the Rajah himself should pay a fine of three crores of rupees for his contumacious conduct. She also asked for the surrender of Mian Jawahir Singh, the second son of Dhyan Singh. Gulab Singh was unwilling to hand over Jawahir Singh to those whose hands were still red with the blood of Dhyan Singh. He sent Jawahir Singh to Jasrota, where Hira Singh had before his death collected an army to attack Chamba. He then ordered all his commanders to be ready with their forces mobilised for action. He recalled even Dewan Hari Chand, whose troops were at Uri, and Wazir Lakhpat, who had gone to Khori for the relief of Gulam Mohiudeen, was also asked to return in haste with the forces at his command. The position was indeed critical. The Lahore Court, which had always been friendly, had become hostile. The Sikh sardars, who never trusted the Jammu rajahs, were ready to wreak vengeance on their supposed disloyalty to Lahore. False rumours were spread and revolt engineered among the Rajputs themselves. But Gulab Singh never lost heart. Sardar Chet Singh of Attari, who was at that time living in Jammu, where he had taken refuge from the hostility of Jindan and her courtiers, tried to placate the Sikh soldiers, but they were bent on attacking Jammu. The Sikh army attacked Jasrota first. Jawahir Singh, who was in charge there, was betrayed by his Dewan, who, with a portion of his army, joined the enemy. Jasrota fell into the hands of Sham Singh, and Jawahir Singh retreated to Jammu. The forces against Gulab Singh gathered strength every day. Faqir-Ullah of Rajauri threw in his lot with the Sikhs and sent a body of soldiers to conquer Poonch. The regiments of Rajah Jawahir Singh at Nowshara mutinied and went over to the enemy. Rajah Lal Singh, the Prime Minister of Lahore, himself took command of the attack, and the Sikh forces even occupied some of the jagirs which had been granted to Gulab Singh. So far the fight had gone against him. The Rajah, however, maintained his courage and put Dewan Hari Chand in charge of the defence of his palace. Wazir Ratanu, who had earned fame in Ladak, and Jawahir Singh were given charge of the defence of Jammu, which was threatened by the Sikh army under Lal Singh. A regiment of Sikhs was at Jasrota, and a force marched down from Ramnagar. The Governor of Kashmir was also ordered by the Lahore Government to send his troops to Khistwar and raise rebellion in that area. Thus surrounded by dangers on all sides a smaller man would have lost heart, but Gulab Singh stood firm. Among those who stood loyally by his side were Dewan Jawala Sahai, his brother Dewan Hari Chand, and Wazir Lakhpat.

Rajah Lal Singh's troops halted at a distance of ten miles from Jammu. As there was no possibility of reducing Jammu, which from its position was considered impregnable, Lal Singh sent Sardar Fateh Singh as emissary to bring Gulab Singh to reason. Gulab Singh said that he was prepared to obey the mandates of the Lahore Government provided his territories were respected. When the emissaries left the palace, Gulab Singh sent Wazir Ratanu with them as escort. But on their way an accident occurred. Some over-zealous soldiers of Rajah Jawahir Singh, who recognised them as sardars of the enemy's camps, shot them while passing the gate. On this, Rajah Lal Singh's troops marched on Jammu. They burnt the villages round about the town, and on the 3rd April, 1845, they invested the town itself. On the Plain of Satwari a battle took place in which the Jammu forces were commanded by Dewan Hari Chand. The Sikh army was defeated and five of their guns fell into the hands of Gulab Singh. But Ramgarh surrendered to the enemy, and though Devigarh was defended heroically by Arjan Mal, it had to yield to superior numbers. At Uttambhai an attempt was made to stop them, but it was not wholly successful. The encircling movement of the Sikh army left Gulab Singh with the option of either withdrawing into the interior or of opening negotiations. He preferred the latter course. The Sikh soldiery was in no mood for peace, but the chiefs persuaded them to retreat to Sialkot. Sardar Sultan Mohammad Khan and Sardar Chattar Singh were deputed to discuss the terms of an armistice. It was suggested that Lal Singh and Gulab Singh should meet and settle the terms of a compromise, and the Lahore chiefs agreed that the Sikhs would return home if Jawahir Singh were surrendered. Gulab Singh agreed, but as soon as the Sikhs got hold of Jawahir Singh they imprisoned him. Bukshi Barkat Ram even then tried to induce the Sikhs to attack the fort, but this scheme was upset by Gulab Singh himself arriving in the Sikh camp with a large retinue. He entrusted Dewan Hari Chand with the government of his State, enjoining him never to yield the fort or city of Jammu. With great courage he then went personally among the Sikh soldiers and won over two regiments to his side. Dewan Jwala Sahai was sent beforehand to the camp of Sardar Mewa Singh Majeetha, who was well known to him. The regiments which Mewa Singh commanded declared themselves in his favour. Gulab Singh distributed money liberally among officers and men, giving to each soldier a present of Rs. 5, and to the general a cash gift of Rs.25,000 and a magnificent horse with saddle of gold and silver. By the same policy he won over some of the minor sardars and a considerable section of the army, which swore on the *Granth*, the Scripture of the Sikhs, that no harm would befall him if he went with them to Lahore. The army chiefs were furious, but the soldiers, without taking any notice of them, returned to Lahore with Gulab Singh at their head.

Rani Jindan was naturally angry when she heard what had happened. She had sent her army to reduce Gulab Singh; she had directed the entire resources of her great State towards this end. But the result was that the enemy whom she was anxious to capture was arriving at the capital at the head of her own army. She sent a message giving expression to her disapproval of the army's conduct, and on this the temper of the soldiers again changed. But General Mewa Singh, with his four regiments, remained true to Gulab Singh, and for the time there was no danger to his life. When the camp reached Shahdara, General Mewa Singh, who went in advance, was imprisoned in the fort by orders of the Queen. Orders were also issued to the soldiers to attack Gulab Singh. The situation was at one time so serious that he thought that his end had come. However, before deciding to give up his life in battle, he decided to outwit the soldiers if possible. Reminding them of their oath on the *Granth* to bring him safely to Lahore, he asked that since they had arrived in Lahore he might be handed over to the Lahore soldiers. To this they agreed. Leaving Dewan Nehal Chand at Shahdara, Gulab Singh, accompanied by Jwala Sahai and Bakhshi Hari Singh, crossed the river and reached Lahore. As soon as the party had crossed, a letter was received ordering the army chiefs to arrest him and bring him under guard to the Durbar. When Gulab Singh reached Lahore a great popular demonstration awaited him. He entered the city half in triumph and half in bondage. He knew that he was a prisoner, but such was the confidence that the masses had in him that they took it for granted that Gulab Singh would come out of all the trouble with flying colours.

On reaching the Durbar he was ordered to be placed in solitary confinement. Dewan Jwala Sahai courageously went to the Durbar and pleaded for honourable treatment for his master. There was still hope left, as Jwala Sahai was free. The Lahore Government desired to obtain Gulab Singh's treasure, and, knowing Jwala Singh to be in the secret, thought of torturing him. But the Dewan was more than a match for the greedy sardars of the

Lahore Court. He spread the news among the soldiers that what the Durbaries wanted was to get for themselves Gulab Singh's hoarded wealth, and to divide his vast possessions amongst themselves. By this method he created an agitation among them. The army chiefs, led by Rattan Singh, waited on Lal Singh and demanded the release of Gulab Singh. Others were also found to give vent to their opinions in open Durbar. The soldiers remembered their oath and declared that if anything happened to Gulab Singh they would take vengeance on the members of the Government. When the attitude of the soldiers came to be known the Government was naturally in a difficult position. They had still another card to play. They produced Dhuleep Singh before the army on the polo ground. But Rattan Singh, who had been well paid by Jwala Sahai, harangued the soldiers beforehand, and when Jawahar Singh appeared on the scene with the young Dhuleep Singh, the soldiers declared unanimously that Gulab Singh should be released. The Durbar was helpless to resist this demand, and Gulab Singh was immediately set free. He was restored to the lands which had been declared forfeited on paying a fine of 68 lakhs, and his lease of the salt mines was renewed. He stayed in Lahore till August, 1845, utilising his time to become popular with the soldiers.

In September, 1845, Jawahar Singh was executed by the soldiers, and the State was again without a minister. Gulab Singh was requested to come and take charge, but the ruler of Jammu could not, after his recent experience and after the treatment meted out to his family, be persuaded to leave his mountain fastness to take part in what had proved for his brothers and nephews a fatal occupation.

Such was the position immediately before the Anglo-Sikh War began. The Lahore Government had made every effort to root out the Jammu family. Only Gulab Singh had escaped from their thirst for blood, and that by sheer good luck. The Khalsa chiefs and Rani Jindan had shown that they bore no good will to Gulab Singh.

CHAPTER V

CONQUEST OF LADAK, BALTISTAN, AND WESTERN TIBET, 1834-1842

THE plateau of Ladak does not belong geographically to India. It forms part of the Himalayan tableland and has for a very long time been ruled by a dynasty which was Tibetan in origin. The population of Ladak is predominantly Mongolian in type. Buddhism in its Lamaistic form is the prevailing religion.

Ladak is bounded on the north by the Karakorum Mountains as far as the Karakorum Pass. On the west it touches Gilgit and Astore. It is one of the most elevated regions in the world, the average height above the sea-level being about 12,000 feet. Enormous mountain peaks ranging from 25,000 to 28,000 feet lend majesty to the ice-clad mountain ranges which encircle it.

The most important portion of Ladak proper is central Ladak, through which runs the River Indus. The climate of Ladak and Baltistan is dry and healthy. During the major portion of the year the weather is intensely cold. The rainfall is very slight and, naturally, vegetation is very scanty. Timber and fuel are the most difficult things to obtain. The population lives by agriculture.

The general aspect of the whole country is thus described by Cunningham in his book *Ladak*, published in 1854:

> The general aspect of Ladak is extreme barrenness. Seen from above it would appear a mere succession of yellow plains and barren mountains capped with snow, and the lakes of Pangkong and Tshomoreri would seem like bright oases in a vast desert of rock and sand. No trace of man or of human habitations would meet the eye, and even the large spots of cultivated land would be but small specks on the mighty waste of a deserted world. But a close view would show many fertile tracts covered with luxuriant crops and picturesque monasteries, from which the chant of human voices ascends high in daily prayer and praise.[1]

Though Baltistan and Ladak are geographically similar and their people ethnologically the same, they follow different religions. The people of Ladak are Buddhists while the people of Baltistan are mainly Mohammadans.

Ladak formed originally a part of Tibet, but in the fifteenth century it became independent under a line of Tibetan kings who accepted the Grand

[1] Cunningham, *Ladak*, p. 16.

Lama as their suzerain. This dynasty continued to rule till the nineteenth century. The last king of this Ladaki dynasty was Tsepal Namgyal, who inherited the throne from his brother. He was an eccentric man, and many stories are told of his peculiarities. He never slept at night nor were any of his servants allowed to do so. It was in his reign that Moorecroft visited Ladak. The English traveller, it would seem, offered to build a fort in Ladak, but Tsepal had wisdom enough to refuse it. Through Moorecroft the Rajah offered to the East India Company an alliance, but for communicating this wish Moorecroft was rebuked by the authorities in Calcutta. The Ladaki chronicles describe the reign of Tsepal as follows:

> Although the land had to suffer much the king did not perceive it, and he never asked whether his subjects fared well or ill. He took an interest only in what concerned his pocket. At that time the royal treasure had increased so much that something had to be done with it and the king decided to use the money for building purposes.

In 1834 Gulab Singh decided to attack Ladak. He made a confidential enquiry of the Company, and, on being informed that the British Government had no objection to his expedition, a well-equipped force was prepared under General Zorawar Singh. This force marched through Kishtwar and entered the Ladaki province of Purig. This province was held by the tri-sultans, whose capital was at Kartse. There was no opposition at first, as the Ladakis were taken by surprise, but about 5,000 men were collected in haste and on the 16th August, 1834, an attempt was made to stop the Dogra advance at Sanku. The Ladakis were heavily defeated. Kartse fell to the Dogras and Zorawar pursued a systematic policy of leaving small garrisons in the forts with a sufficient supply of arms.

From Kartse the invading army marched down the Suru River. On the plains of Pashkyum the Ladakis were again defeated. As winter was approaching, Zorawar, anxious to return to a warmer climate, entered into negotiations. But the Ladakis, depending upon the extreme cold of the winter to drive away Zorawar's men, refused to negotiate and took to guerilla warfare. Moreover, they also set themselves to collect an army with which to fight the Dogras. By the time their preparations were over winter had lost its rigours. The Ladaki army marched to Langkartse, where the Dogras had encamped for winter. But the army that had been collected with so much difficulty did not fight. The

Dogras watched for a few days the camps of their enemies, and, finding that they were not exerting themselves, attacked them. No effort was made by the Ladakis to defend their positions. They merely ran away, and in their flight the snow of their country inflicted untold misery. After this Zorawar had but little fighting to do. The Ladaki army retreated to Leh. Tsepal lost heart and agreed to negotiate, and himself came to Bazgo, where a meeting took place between Zorawar and the King. After the terms were settled Zorawar went up to Leh and installed Tsepal as a ruler holding power from Gulab Singh. He was asked to pay an annual tribute of Rs.20,000 and a war indemnity of Rs.50,000. After making peace Zorawar returned to Lamayura.

The Sikhs, who were jealous of Gulab Singh's growing power, looked upon Zorawar's conquest with envy. At the instigation of Mihan Singh, the Governor of Kashmir, the Ladakis rose in revolt, and the Dogra garrison in Suru was put to death. The cold season had set in and snow had closed the passes. But Zorawar was not the man to wait. By forced marches he arrived at Leh, to the utter surprise of his enemies. The Gyalpo expressed remorse at what had taken place, but Zorawar inflicted exemplary punishment on the rebels. Placing sufficient garrisons in the forts and leaving an agent, Dewan Daya Ram, with the King, Zorawar returned to Jammu for the winter. The next year Zorawar returned to Leh to find Tsepal at the head of a rebellion engineered by the Sikhs in Kashmir. Tsepal was deposed and was given merely the village of Stog, where his descendants still live with the nominal title of Gyalpo. In his place Ngroub Stanzan, a relation of the old King, was made Governor of Ladak. This time, however, Zorawar did not want to take anything on trust. He fortified Leh and placed a garrison there. Next year Zorawar again appeared on the scene, deposed Ngroub Stanzan, who was accused of rebellion, and reinstalled Tsepal at an increased tribute.

The country, though conquered, had not yet settled down. By the end of 1840 the Ladakis found a leader in a man called Sukamir. Before the rebellion could mature Zorawar again appeared with a sufficient force. The rebel leader was caught and publicly executed. This created sufficient fear in the mind of the Ladakis, who have since peacefully accepted the rule of Dogras over their country.

Having thus finally conquered Ladak, Zorawar turned his attention towards Baltistan. Though the people of Baltistan are of the same stock as the Ladakis, they are, as has already been mentioned, Mohammadans by religion. The leading chief of the Balti country was the Sultan of Skardo. Mohammad Shah, the eldest son of the reigning ruler, requested Zorawar's help to get his claims recognised. Zorawar organised a Ladaki army under their own generals, and with the help of this force invaded Baltistan. The Balti army was defeated and the fort of Skardo was taken. Mohammad Shah, the disinherited son, was made sultan, but Zorawar was careful enough to leave a Dogra garrison to support his authority. In this campaign the Ladakis played a notable part, and King Tsepal, who had never before fought a campaign even to save his own kingdom, accompanied Zorawar. On his return from the campaign the old King died and a grandson of his, a boy aged eight years, was acknowledged as Gyalpo.

Zorawar was not satisfied with these conquests. He now undertook a more difficult, and as it turned out a disastrous, expedition. During the long history of India no army from Hindustan had attacked Tibet. No Indian ruler had thought of conquering it and no Indian general accustomed to the heat of the plains had ever dared to face the rigour of the Tibetan climate. Zorawar conceived the idea of conquering the central Tibetan province for his master and prepared an expedition for that purpose.

In May, 1841, he advanced up the Indus and conquered Rudok and Garo. From there he advanced into the district of Mansarawara. So far there had been no opposition. His army consisted only of 5,000 soldiers, most of whom were Balti and Ladaki recruits, stiffened by a small Dogra force.

The country was overrun. Zorawar himself camped at Tirthapuri while Colonel Baste Ram, who is the chronicler of the campaign, was stationed at Takla Gor on the Nepal frontier. Zorawar had not expected that any serious attempt would be made by the Tibetans during the winter, but in this he was wrong. It was in November, 1841, when the cold of Tibet had already become unbearable, that Zorawar heard that a Lhassa force was approaching to meet the invaders. A small detachment which he had sent to oppose the enemy forces and to find out their strength was cut to pieces by the Tibetans. A second force, which was sent under Gulam Khan, met with no better fate.

It was then that Zorawar realised the danger. Retreat through the snows was impossible, and the enemy who was facing him was more than twice the number he had under his command. Accepting the Napoleonic maxim that attack was the best form of defence, he advanced with his whole available force to meet the enemy. The battle commenced on the 10th December, 1841, and continued for three days. On the 12th Zorawar was wounded by a bullet, and, though he fought like a lion even after this, a Tibetan warrior pierced him through the breast with his lance.

Thus died Zorawar Singh, a soldier of whose achievements India could justly be proud. Besides being an intrepid commander, as the Ladak and Baltistan campaign had shown him to be, he was also gifted with considerable political ability. His settlement of the newly conquered provinces bears witness to this. To have marched an army not once or twice, but six times over the snow-clad ranges of Ladak and Baltistan, 15,000 feet above sea-level, where the air is so rarefied that people from the plains can hardly live with comfort, is a wonderful achievement. To have conquered that country after successive campaigns and reduced it to a peaceful province is an exploit for which there is no parallel in Indian history. His greatness will shine through the pages of Indian history as that of a great and noble warrior.

'The Indian soldiers of Zorawar Singh,' says Cunningham, 'fought under very great disadvantages. The battlefield was upwards of 15,000 feet above the sea and the time mid-winter, when even during the day the temperature never rises above the freezing point and the intense cold of night can only be borne by people well covered with sheepskins and surrounded by fires. For several nights the Indian troops had been exposed to all the bitternesses of the climate. Many had lost the use of their fingers and toes; and all were more or less frost-bitten . . . on the last fatal day not one-half of the men could handle arms."[1]

When Zorawar marched into Tibet the British Government became anxious. The King of Lahore, Sher Singh, was therefore asked that Gulab Singh should be requested to evacuate Lhassa territories. The date was actually fixed (10th December, 1841), and Captain Cunningham, the historian of the Sikhs, who was assistant to the British Agent, was selected to proceed to Ladak in order to witness the evacuation of Tibetan territory. But before the orders reached Zorawar disaster had overtaken him.

After Zorawar's death the Dogra army suffered untold hardship and a great portion of it was annihilated. Of the 5,000 men not more than 1,000 escaped. The political reaction on Ladak was great. The Ladakis rose in revolt, and the Tibetans sent a force to help them. But though Zorawar was killed and a whole army was destroyed, Gulab Singh did not lose heart. Misfortune only steeled him to greater efforts. A new army was immediately raised and despatched under Dewan Hari Chand and Wazir Ratanu. This was even better equipped than the army of Zorawar. With the approach of the Dogra force the Tibetans fled in

[1] Cunningham, *Ladak*, p. 353.

the direction of the Shyok. The Dogra leaders occupied Leh.

The Tibetans, however, were not prepared to give in without a fight. A strong Tibetan force of 3,000 men was sent by the Lhassa authorities to help the Ladakis. The contending armies met at Drangtse, where the Tibetans had entrenched themselves. Finding them occupying positions which it was difficult to carry by assault, the Dogras dammed up a river and flooded their entrenchments and thus forced them out of their strong positions. A fierce battle took place outside the entrenchments and the Tibetans were defeated. Their general was captured and killed on the spot. On this, the Lhassa Government agreed to seek peace and the following treaty[1] was signed:

> Whereas we the Officers of the Lhassa country, viz., firstly, Kalon Sukanwala, and, secondly, Bakhshi Sapju, Commander of the Forces of the Empire of China, on the one hand, and Dewan Hari Chand and Wazir Ratanu, on behalf of Rajah Gulab Singh, on the other—agree together and swear before God that the friendship between Rajah Gulab Singh and the Emperor of China and the

[1] Translation of the Persian copy, reproduced in *Gulabnama,* p. 264.

Lama Guru Sahib Lassawalla will be kept and observed till eternity; no disregard will be shown to anything agreed upon in the presence of God; and we will have nothing to do with the countries bordering on the frontier of Ladak. We will carry on the trade in Shawl, Pasham, and Tea as before by way of Ladak; and if any one of the Shri Rajah's enemies comes to our territories and says anything against the Rajah we will not listen to him, and will not allow him to remain in our country, and whatever traders come from Ladak shall experience no difficulty from our side. We will not act otherwise but in the same manner as it has been prescribed in this meeting regarding the fixing of the Ladak frontier and the keeping open of the road for the traffic in Shawl, Pasham, and Tea. We will observe our pledge to God, Gaitri, and Pasi. Wazir Mian Khushal Chu is witness.

Written on the second day of Assuj, 1899 (about 15th August, 1842).

The Tibetan version of the treaty is as follows:

Kalon Surkhan and investigating officer Depon Pishi on behalf of His Holiness the Dalai Lama and his officials, and Shri Khalsaji Absarani Shri Maharajah, Lala Golana, the representative of Khashur Shag Golam Mohammed through an interpreter Amirshah (on behalf of Gulab Singh) have arrived at Ladak and discussed the terms of the peace treaty. In the first place the two contracting parties have decided to sink all past differences and ill-feeling and to consider the friendship and unity between the two Kings re-established for ever. This peace treaty between Shri Maharajah Gulab Singh and Shri Guru Lama of Lhassa has been restored and there will be no cause for enmity in future in the two nations regarding their respective frontier. Shri Maharajah Sahib has declared, invoking God as his witness, that he will not deviate from the terms of this agreement. It is agreed that the two brothers Kings of Ladak and the Queen shall remain peacefully in Ladak and shall not indulge in any intrigue, besides trying to promote the friendly relations between the two nations. The Ladakis shall send the annual tribute to His Holiness the Dalai Lama and his Ministers unfailingly as heretofore and the Shri Maharajah Sahib will not interfere with this arrangement. No restriction shall be laid on the mutual export and import of commodities—*e.g.*, tea, piece goods, etc.—and trading shall be allowed according to the old-established custom. The Ladakis shall supply the Tibetan Government traders with the usual transport animals and arrange for their accommodation as heretofore, and the Tibetans will also do the same to the Ladakis who come to Tibet with the annual tribute. It is agreed that no trouble will be occasioned to the Tibetan Government by the Ladakis. We invoke God to bear witness to this agreement whereby the friendly relations between the Shri Maharajah Sahib and the Lhassa officials shall continue as between members of the same family. This is sent on the second day of the month of Assuj, year 1899.

As this treaty was between Gulab Singh and the Lhassa Government and did not bind the suzerains of both, a further treaty on behalf of the Government of Lahore and the Emperor of China seems to have been negotiated almost immediately.

The following is the translation from the Tibetan of that treaty:

In these auspicious days we the officials of Shri Maharajah Sahib, the Commander-in-Chief of the Western area in the Court of Shri

Rajah Gulab Singh, and we the trusted and selected and the faithfully loyal Itamad-ud-Dowlah Nizam-ul-Mulik Sheikh Ghulam Mohiyuddin Subedar (Governor) of Kashmir, met together on the second of Assuj, 1899, the officials of the Lama Guru Sahib of Lhassa, one of them Kalan Sokan and the other Depon Shabeho *Bakshi* in Ladak and, having settled differences, a treaty was recorded as in the past (to the following effect):

Now that in the presence of God the ill-feeling created by the war which had intervened, has been fully removed from the hearts, and no complaints now remain (on either side), there will never be on any account in future, while the world lasts, any deviation even by the hair's breadth or any breach in the alliance, friendship, and unity between the King of the World (Sher Singh) Sri Khalsaji Sahib (and Gulab Singh) Sri Maharaja Sahib Raja-i-Rajgan Raja Sahib Bahadur, and the Khagan (Emperor) of China and the Lama Guru Sahib of Lhassa. We shall remain in possession of the limits of the boundaries of Ladak and the neighbourhood subordinate to it, in accordance with the old customs, and there shall be no transgression and no interference in the country beyond the old-established frontiers.

We shall hold to our own respective frontiers, relations of friendship and the bond of common interests shall grow closer from day to day. There are several kinds of witnesses to this agreement. The Rajah Zadas shall, if they remain faithful, loyal, and obedient receive greater consideration. Traders from Lhassa when they come to Ladak shall, as of old, receive considerate treatment and a supply of begar (transport and labour). In case the Rajahs of Ladak should [desire to] send their usual presents to the Lama Guru Sahib of Lhassa, this will not concern us and we shall not interfere. From the other side [arrangements] shall continue in accordance with the old custom and the traders who proceed to Janthan (Cheng Thang) country shall receive considerate treatment and a supply of begar in accordance with the old custom and shall not be interfered with. The traders from Ladak shall in no case interfere with the subjects of Janthan (Chang Thang).

Written on the second of the month of Assuj, year 1899.

CHAPTER VI

GULAB SINGH AND THE SIKH WAR

It is not necessary for the purpose of this memoir to describe the reasons of the Anglo-Sikh war and the campaign on the Sutlej.

On the 8th November, 1845, Lal Singh assumed the post of Prime Minister of the Lahore State and Tej Singh was appointed Commander-in-Chief of the Sikh army. The Sikh soldiers did not like the appointment of Tej Singh and clamoured for Gulab Singh to lead them.[1] But the ruler of Jammu was away in the hills and Lal Singh was anxious that he should be sent to the Afghan frontier. The Sikhs crossed the Sutlej, as they had become convinced that the British Government intended to annex the Punjab. The campaign which opened was not so easy as the British Government had expected. In the open field the Sikhs proved their prowess, but if they had hoped for victories they were soon disillusioned. If there had been unity of command or vigour of action on the Sikh side the British would have been faced with a grave

[1] Governor-General to the Secret Committee. Dated 4th December, 1845. Parliamentary Papers. Papers respecting the late hostilities on the North-West Frontiers.

danger to their Empire. The only person who could have given the Sikhs the lead they required at the time was Gulab Singh. Unfortunately, after his own experience and the fate that overtook the rest of his family, that chief was in no hurry to come to the help of the Lahore Government. As soon as the war broke out the Lahore Government ordered Gulab Singh to proceed to Peshawar and hold the frontier. In reply, Gulab Singh urged the Queen not to interfere in the affairs of the British. Gulab Singh wrote also to the Council of Regency as follows:

> The British authorities have not acted contrary to the agreement. Neither have they broken their word. So to fight them without any reason is wrong. Though you killed my brothers and their sons without reason, who had been loyal subjects and faithful servants of the departed Majesty, I have the same feeling of loyalty to His present Majesty. I cannot question your right to do whatever you please within your territories in his name. But do not interfere in the affairs of the British.

This advice was not heeded and the Regency rushed headlong into war. When it was found that the campaign would be arduous and, if the sovereignty of the Punjab was not to be lost, sustained efforts would be required, the Regency invited Gulab Singh to come and take charge of the Government as Prime Minister. Gulab Singh, knowing that the time had not come for his effective intervention, went on a pilgrimage to Trikuti and from there went to Reasi. His excuse was that he had not been summoned by the Queen.

When the campaign was going against the Sikhs and the demand for his return was unanimous, Gulab Singh arrived in Lahore. When his forces arrived near Lahore the Queen sent Bhai Ram Singh and Dewan Dina Nath to receive and escort him to the capital. On 27th January, 1846, he was installed as Prime Minister. Gulab Singh reproached the Sikh leaders for entering on so serious a campaign without securing unity at home, and advised that an effort should be made to secure as honourable a peace as possible before it became too late. With this object he immediately entered into negotiations with the British Government. The Governor-General and the British Army chiefs, who had underestimated the strength and skill of the Sikh army, welcomed Gulab Singh's effort to settle the issue by diplomacy. All their ideas of dictating a treaty at Lahore had vanished when it was found that there was a difficult campaign before them. In agreeing to negotiate they made a condition that the army should be disbanded. To this Gulab Singh would not agree. Cunningham accuses the Sikh leaders of a secret agreement that the army in the field would be abandoned when the fight began and that the passage of the Sutlej would be unopposed and the road to Lahore left open. There is nothing to prove this allegation of disgraceful treachery on the part of the Sikh commanders.

On the 10th February, 1846, the Battle of Sobraon was fought. This was the most fiercely contested battle that the English had ever fought in India. The Sikhs fought with undaunted courage, and the victory of the British, though decisive, was dearly bought. Their casualties numbered 320 killed and 2,083 wounded.

After this Gulab Singh was given full powers to negotiate with the British. He sent three messengers—Lala Chouri Mal Harkara, Haski, and Lala Anant Ram—to the camp of the British Governor-General.

The necessity of conciliating Gulab Singh at this critical time was realised by the British. His army was intact, and if he had decided to put his resources and force at the disposal of the Lahore Government the issue would again have become doubtful. It was reported that Gulab Singh had advised that the British could have been kept in check if the Sikhs, instead of trying to force issues by open pitched battles, had crossed the Sutlej with a few picked cavalry regiments and had attempted to strike at Delhi. The British authorities, who knew the force of this advice, were naturally anxious to conciliate Gulab Singh, and when his emissaries reached the British camp the following letter was sent by Sir Henry Lawrence, whose friendship with the Rajah was well known:

KIND RAJAH SAHIB AND DEAR FRIEND,

Please accept my best wishes and kindest regards. I received your kind letter. Let me explain the matter to you. I appreciate all that you have written wisely and prudently. Although it is difficult to know the rebels and non-rebels, the British Government wants to show forbearance to the Lahore Durbar. The Government does not at all feel happy at the anarchy and misgovernment of the Lahore State. The intention of the Company is only to punish the rebels so that in future there should be no misdeeds. I have explained the situation to Anant Ram, who will himself relate it to you. In case of delay matters will grow worse. You know that every time the Sikhs encountered the British they were defeated. If even now they are left unpunished, and there be any such trouble again,

> it will then be worse for the Durbar of Lahore. You will, I believe, know from this letter that, in spite of all that has occurred, we have still the same feeling and sympathy for the Lahore Durbar. I hope you will always favour me with your kind letters and friendly communications.

This communication was a diplomatic one meant to assure Gulab Singh of the personal friendliness of the British Government without committing the authorities to any proposal beyond that of sympathy to the Lahore Durbar. But other questions were being discussed behind the scenes with a view to securing the co-operation of Gulab Singh, as will be evident from the following letter written two days later by Sir Henry Lawrence (13th February, 1846):

> KIND RAJAH SAHIB AND DEAR FRIEND,
>
> Receive my regards and let it be known to you that I want to say to you a word which will be to your utmost good. So I hope you may manage to hear it from me personally. Do this please, and do this without delay. I hope you will remember me with your friendly letter.

This cryptic and mysterious note, it need not be said, was the invitation to consider proposals intended to separate Gulab Singh from his allegiance to the Lahore State. The private proposals which Lawrence wanted to place before Gulab Singh were that he should be recognised as independent and Kashmir be added to his territory if he withdrew his support from the Lahore Government. A conference was held, and, when the general proposals with regard to the treaty with Lahore were being discussed, Lawrence took Gulab Singh aside for a private conversation. The following version of what occurred is that of Dewan Kripa Ram, who was a trusted servant of Gulab Singh and, later, occupied the position of Prime Minister of Jammu and Kashmir.

Lawrence reminded Gulab Singh of his troubles with the Lahore Durbar, how he had lost his brothers and his nephew in the anarchy that followed Ranjit Singh's death, and expressed astonishment at the devotion which the Rajah was showing. He told him that the Governor-General had promised to grant him the hilly district, together with the country of Kashmir, after having separated them from the Government of the Punjab, and that Gulab Singh would be recognised as an independent ruler.

Gulab Singh, in reply, said that if the Lahore

Government had treated his brothers and nephew badly they were, after all, the subjects of Lahore, and that in no case could any blame attach to Dhuleep Singh, who was at the time a child, and that, as he came as envoy, he could not negotiate about his own possessions. This was reported to the Governor-General and the matter was dropped for the time. The negotiations on behalf of the Lahore Government were continued, and Gulab Singh was able to secure for his Sovereign what was in the circumstances a reasonably moderate treaty.

This treaty recognised Dhuleep Singh as ruler, but required that the country between Beas and Sutlej should be handed over to the British and that £1,500,000 sterling should be paid as indemnity. The conditions were agreed to by Gulab Singh on behalf of the Lahore Government, and on the 20th February, 1846, the British Army reached Lahore. The success of Gulab Singh in negotiating this treaty infuriated Lal Singh, who persuaded the Regent to withdraw his authority and to appoint himself as Wazir. It was then that Gulab Singh realised the precariousness of his position. He had not accepted the British proposal of independence but had remained loyal to the Lahore Government. But the dissolute Regent and her paramour, though they sent for him at the time of disaster, still cherished that violent animosity towards the Jammu family which had been responsible for the murders of Dhyan Singh, Suchet Singh, and Hira Singh. He was deprived of the wazirat by the elevation of Lal Singh to the post.

Lal Singh, in accepting the treaty negotiated at Kasaur, protested his inability to pay the £1,500,000 sterling demanded as indemnity in cash, and offered to hand over Jammu and Kashmir. His idea was to deprive Gulab Singh of his territory and give the British the option either of holding Kashmir, which would have been impossible at that time, or of accepting a reduced indemnity. This offer of Lal Singh suited the Jammu ruler, and the original proposal to make Gulab Singh the independent ruler of Jammu and Kashmir was revived. This time, however, there was a condition attached to it—namely, that Gulab Singh should pay the indemnity which had been made a charge on the territory by the cleverness of Lal Singh.

Gulab Singh agreed to pay the money, and the Governor-General on his side agreed to recognise him as an independent Sovereign. When the Queen Regent heard of this, she sent Dewan Dina Nath, Fakeer Anwaruddin, and Bhai Ram Singh to Sir Henry Lawrence and told him that if it was intended to implement this proposal she would appeal to Queen Victoria direct. This intervention of the Regent had no effect and the Treaty of

Lahore was signed as originally negotiated by Gulab Singh.

The treaty with the Lahore Durbar, which was signed on the 9th March, 1846, had a clause to the following effect:

> In consideration of the services rendered by Rajah Gulab Singh of Jammu to the Lahore State towards procuring the restoration of the relations of amity between the Lahore and British Governments, the Maharajah (Dhuleep Singh) hereby agrees to recognise the independent sovereignty of Rajah Gulab Singh in such territories and districts in the hills as may be made over to the said Rajah Gulab Singh by separate agreement between himself and the British Government with dependencies thereof which may have been in the Rajah's possession since the time of Maharajah Kharrak Singh and the British Government in consideration of the good conduct of Rajah Gulab Singh also *agrees to recognise his independence* in such territories and to admit him to the privilege of a separate Treaty with the British Government.

On the 16th March, 1846, seven days after the Treaty of Lahore, Maharajah Gulab Singh of

Jammu signed the Treaty of Amritsar, by which he became the Maharajah of Jammu and Kashmir. The Valley of Kashmir, famous all over the world and sacred in Hindu mythology, became again an independent State.

The 'sale' of Kashmir to Gulab Singh has of late been attacked as a foolish and short-sighted policy by men who now realise how that cool and temperate valley could have been utilised as a British Colony. But in discussing this question there has been much misunderstanding of historical facts. The view that Kashmir was sold for a paltry sum by a Government whose main interest was to fill its coffers is a travesty of facts and a misreading of history.

The following letter written by Lord Hardinge to Lord Ellenborough in justification of his action gives in detail the considerations that led the Governor-General to conclude the Treaty of Amritsar. Lord Hardinge writes:

> Gulab Singh was never Minister of Lahore for the administration of its affairs. Early in 1845 Jowahir Singh persuaded the army to march against Jammu. Gulab Singh, despairing of being able to defend himself, threw himself into the hands of the Panchayats and was brought a prisoner to Lahore. He was

there treated with great severity; and, subsequently, when the army offered him the Wazirship, he repeatedly declined the offer. When the invasion took place he remained at Jammu and took no part against us, but tendered his allegiance on condition of being confirmed in the possession of his own territories. This was neither conceded nor refused, as the Paramount Power did not think it becoming, while the armies were in presence of each other, to show any doubt as to the result by granting terms. I merely referred him to the terms of the Proclamation of December, when the Sikhs crossed Sutlej. Nevertheless, it was clearly to be understood by the terms of that Proclamation that if Gulab Singh took no part against us he was entitled to consideration whenever the affairs of the Punjab came to be settled. It was evident that he had no cause for gratitude or attachment to the Lahore Durbar, by whose orders and intrigues his own family had been nearly exterminated, his possessions taken, and his sons slain. During the whole of the campaign he had purposely kept aloof; not a single hill soldier had fired a shot against us, so that the Government had every right to treat with him. They had their own interest, also, to attend to, which required that the Sikh State should be weakened and that the hills should be separated from the plains.

Were we to be deterred from doing what was right and what had been previously determined upon, because the Lahore Durbar, knowing he had not participated in their crime, chose to employ him for a particular object as being the man most acceptable to us? Was he not the Minister, and were not four other Commissioners associated with him for settling the terms of peace? After Mudki and Feroz Shah, the Rani had implored him to come to Lahore and bring his troops to her aid. He sent evasive answers. After the battle of Aliwal more pressing invitations were sent, as he alone, in their opinion, could settle affairs with the English, because he had not taken part against them. He came to Lahore protesting publicly in Durbar against all that had been done. He accepted the responsibility of attempting a settlement, but required the Rani to sign a paper that she would accede to the terms which he and the other four Commissioners should agree upon. He had been told by Major Lawrence on the 3rd February in a written document that he appreciated his wisdom in not having taken up arms against us and that his interests would be taken into consideration. The words of the Proclamation, dated 14th February, were these:

'The extent of the territory which it may be advisable to take will be determined by the conduct of the Durbar and by consideration for the security of the British Frontier.'

These words were meant to include any arrangements which would render the hills independent of the plain, which arrangement had been well considered before the battle of Sobraon. It was always intended that Gulab Singh, whose troops had not fired a shot, should have his case and position fully considered. What act of treason, then, had he committed against the Lahore State? He had done good service to us, which we had recognised before he was a Sikh Commissioner. After the war commenced were we to abandon our policy and to treat the only man who had not lifted up his arms against us with indifference because he came to Headquarters specially deputed by the Lahore Durbar to confer with us as one who had not joined in their unprovoked invasion? His forbearance was rewarded because his forbearance was in accordance with an intended policy, and because the charge of treachery could not be substantiated.

In discussing this question of the transfer of Kashmir, it is also important to remember that there was no sale of Kashmir at all. Clause 12 of the Treaty of Lahore with Maharajah Dhuleep Singh, then an independent ruler, shows clearly that even before the treaty with Lahore was signed it was agreed that the areas surrendered by the Lahore Government between Ravi and the Indus were to be transferred to Gulab Singh. What Lal Singh did was to make over Jammu, Kashmir, and all the territories between the Ravi and the Indus to the Company, thus giving away Ladak, Baltistan, and other areas which belonged to Gulab Singh instead of paying £1,500,000 sterling demanded as war indemnity. By doing this he cleverly created a charge on the territory which was already promised to Gulab Singh for his services in procuring the restoration of the relations of amity between the Lahore and British Governments. It should clearly be understood that the Treaty of Amritsar does not stand by itself. It is to be read along with the Treaty of Lahore, which will make it clear that Kashmir was not sold.

It is also clear from the narrative of the negotiations given in this chapter that the cession of Kashmir was the price paid for Gulab Singh's efforts to bring about a speedy peace which, if he had thrown in his weight with the Lahore Durbar, would not have been an easy matter to achieve. The ease with which the peace was concluded was due to the agreement reached with Gulab Singh by which Kashmir had already been promised to him.

Further, it should be remembered that it would have been impossible at the time for the East India Company to conquer Kashmir. It should be remembered that the British boundary in 1845 was the Sutlej. The Lahore kingdom had not been annexed and it would not have been possible to annex it at that time without a more arduous campaign. Though they had been defeated at Sobraon, the spirit of the Khalsa was not yet broken, and if there had been any attempt to annex the Punjab another campaign would have been required, for which the Company was not yet prepared. With their base at Firozepur, a hostile Punjab on the line of communications, and the Sikhs ready to rise, it would have been impossible for the British in 1845 either to undertake the conquest of Kashmir or to hold it if conquered. It is purely a vain retrospective regret which sees in the acquisition of Kashmir by Gulab Singh a short-sighted policy meant to enrich the coffers of the Company.

In the eighteenth century and long after it Kashmir was not considered a part of India. Till Ranjit Singh conquered it, Kashmir was an Afghan province, and in all the schemes for the partition of the Punjab which were discussed, there were many proposals which allotted Peshawar and other areas, now considered to be integral parts of India, to Afghan princes. Kashmir was also considered foreign territory. Therefore the Government of India, even if we could impute nationalist motives to it at the time, could not feel any difficulty on that score.

One of the main objects which the Government of India had in view was to reduce the area and resources of the Sikh empire, which, when it extended from Multan to Gilgit, was indeed a serious power. By the dismemberment of the empire this object was realised.

Writing to a near relative, Lord Hardinge gives the following reason for the transfer of Kashmir, which makes the above point of view clear:

> It was necessary last March to weaken the Sikhs by depriving them of Kashmir. The distance from Kashmir to the Sutlej is 300 miles of very difficult mountainous country quite impracticable for six months. To keep a British force 300 miles from any possibility of support would have been an undertaking

> that merited a strait-waistcoat and not a peerage. The arrangement made was the only alternative. The Government took away with one hand and gave with the other as the exigencies of the case required; and as regards the honesty of the transaction, the names of Currie and Lawrence as a sufficient guarantee. Gulab Singh's character was not without reproach; but where was the native chief or minister to be found without similar blots on his escutcheon.[1]

Sir George Clerk, who was for a very long time the Agent to the Governor-General at Lahore, wrote to Sir Charles Napier as follows in March, 1849:

> I have been under the necessity on more than one occasion of testing rather severely Goolab Singh's loyalty to us. My belief is that *he is a man eminently qualified by character* and surrounding territorial possessions for the position of ruler there, that all his interests lie on the side of friendship with us, that he will always desire and sometime or another may need our countenance of his authority against enemies. Their aggressions, whether Chinese or Goorkhas on one side of him or

[1] *Life of Lord Hardinge,* p. 133. (Oxford, 1891.)

> Afghans on the other, will be retarded rather than precipitated by his proximity to them in that form *instead of our being in more direct* contact with them.

Sir George added that Ranjit Singh 'fostered in the north of his kingdom a Rajput power because it could have no affinity with his turbulent Khalsa on one side or with malignant and vindictive Islam on the other. Had proof of the wisdom of this measure been wanting, it has been signally shown in his time and in ours on four important occasions. Lord Hardinge gave still greater substance to that Hill ruler. The measure was provident and wise. There are those who now would disregard his policy and who seem to be utterly ignorant of the motives of it.'

That the Government of India was fully alive to these considerations may be seen from the fact that the Governor-General in his despatch to the Secret Committee discusses these points in detail.[1] It was not without a full examination of all the relevant facts that the agreement by which Gulab Singh received the addition of Kashmir to his territories was signed, and it is not for those who benefited by his action in 1845 to express regret now and allege that the agreement was not a fair bargain. Retro-

[1] See Appendix I.

spectively, it is easy to brush aside these considerations by a facile confusion of thought and to state how much better it would have been for the British to have kept Kashmir and not to have 'sold' it for cash.

It is possible to hold two views about Gulab Singh's attitude during the Sikh war. It is undoubtedly true that he had been for years cultivating the friendship of the British Government. It is also equally true that when the war broke out between the Company and the Sikhs he did not hasten with his forces to the standard of his Sovereign, but held back in Jammu and even went on a pilgrimage to Trikuti. It is also undeniable that when he did take charge of the Lahore Government in January, 1846, he could, by his ability and prestige and the resources at his command, have prolonged the war and caused infinite trouble to the British. In fact, at Kassur he actually gave out that he knew the strength of his position.

There is, therefore, a *prima facie* case for the belief that Gulab Singh had already agreed with the British authorities that he would remain neutral in the conflict. Considering the treatment meted out to him and his family, few will condemn Gulab Singh's action. His brothers and nephews had been mercilessly done to death. Only a few months before he himself was publicly humiliated and imprisoned. The persistent hostility of the Lahore Durbar towards him and his family had been clear for many years. That even under this provocation he had not been actively hostile to the Lahore Government but had remained neutral speaks well for Gulab Singh's loyalty to the memory of Ranjit Singh. Up to the very last he endeavoured to secure the best terms possible for Dhuleep Singh. It is, therefore, impossible to accuse him of anything like active treachery to the Sikhs.

CHAPTER VII

TREATY OF AMRITSAR AND THE FOUNDATION OF THE STATE

THE text of the Treaty of Amritsar is as follows:

TREATY BETWEEN THE BRITISH GOVERNMENT on the one part and MAHARAJAH GULAB SINGH OF JAMMU on the other concluded on the part of the BRITISH GOVERNMENT by FREDERICK CURRIE, Esquire, and BREVET-MAJOR HENRY MONTGOMERY LAWRENCE, acting under the orders of the RIGHT HONOURABLE SIR HENRY HARDINGE, G.C.B., one of HER BRITANNIC MAJESTY'S MOST HONOURABLE PRIVY COUNCIL, GOVERNOR-GENERAL of the possessions of the EAST INDIA COMPANY, to direct and control all their affairs in the EAST INDIES and by MAHARAJAH GULAB SINGH in person—1846.

ARTICLE 1

The British Government transfers and makes over for ever in independent possession to Maharajah Gulab Singh and the heirs male of his body all the hilly or mountainous country with its dependencies situated to the eastward of the River Indus and the westward of the River Ravi including Chamba and excluding Lahul, being part of the territories ceded to the British Government by the Lahore State according to the provisions of Article IV. of the Treaty of Lahore, dated 9th March, 1846.

ARTICLE 2

The eastern boundary of the tract transferred by the foregoing article to Maharajah Gulab Singh shall be laid down by the Commissioners appointed by the British Government and Maharajah Gulab Singh respectively for that purpose and shall be defined in a separate engagement after survey.

ARTICLE 3

In consideration of the transfer made to him and his heirs by the provisions of the foregoing article Maharajah Gulab Singh will pay to the British Government the sum of seventy-five Lakhs of Rupees (Nanukshahee), fifty lakhs to be paid on ratification of this Treaty and twenty-five lakhs on or before the 1st October of the current year, A.D. 1846.

ARTICLE 4

The limits of the territories of Maharajah Gulab Singh shall not be at any time changed without concurrence of the British Government.

ARTICLE 5

Maharajah Gulab Singh will refer to the arbitration of the British Government any disputes or questions that may arise between himself and the Government of Lahore or any other neighbouring State, and will abide by the decision of the British Government.

ARTICLE 6

Maharajah Gulab Singh engages for himself and heirs to join, with the whole of his Military Forces, the British troops, when employed within the hills or in the territories adjoining his possessions.

ARTICLE 7

Maharajah Gulab Singh engages never to take or retain in his service any British subject nor the subject of any European or American State without the consent of the British Government.

ARTICLE 8

Maharajah Gulab Singh engages to respect in regard to the territory transferred to him, the provisions of Articles V., VI., and VII., of the separate Engagement between the British Government and the Lahore Durbar, dated 11th March, 1846.[1]

[1] Referring to jagirdars, arrears of revenue and the property in the forts that are to be transferred.

Article 9

The British Government will give its aid to Maharajah Gulab Singh in protecting his territories from external enemies.

Article 10

Maharajah Gulab Singh acknowledges the supremacy of the British Government and will in token of such supremacy present annually to the British Government one horse, twelve shawl goats[1] of approved breed (six male and six female) and three pairs of Cashmere shawls.

This Treaty of ten articles has been this day settled by Frederick Currie, Esquire, and Brevet-Major Henry Montgomery Lawrence, acting under directions of The Right Honourable Sir Henry Hardinge, G.C.B., Governor-General, on the part of the British Government and by Maharajah Gulab Singh in person, and the said Treaty has been this day ratified by the seal of The Right Honourable Sir Henry Hardinge, G.C.B., Governor-General.

(Done at Amritsar the sixteenth day of March,

[1] On the 13th March, 1884, it was arranged by mutual consent that in future the Maharajah should present, instead of 12 goats, 10 lbs. of pashm in its natural state as brought to Kashmir from Leh, 4 lbs. of picked and assorted black wool, 4 lbs. grey wool, 4 lbs. white wool, and 1 lb. of each of the three best qualities of white yarn.

in the year of our Lord one thousand eight hundred and forty-six, corresponding with the seventeenth day of Rubee-ul-Awal 1262 Jijree).

(*Signed*) H. HARDINGE (Seal).

(*Signed*) F. CURRIE.
(*Signed*) H. M. LAWRENCE.

By Order of the Right Honourable the Governor-General of India.

(*Signed*) F. CURRIE,
Secretary to the Government of India, with the Governor-General.

This treaty stands on a different footing from other treaties with Indian States. The territories of which the Maharajah was recognised as ruler were handed over to him in independent possession. While the supremacy of the British Government was acknowledged there was no agreement on the part of the Company to guarantee the internal security of the State, Article 9 merely binding the British authorities to give aid to Maharajah Gulab Singh in protecting his territories from external aggression.

The sum to be paid by the Maharajah was fixed at one crore of rupees (10,000,000). Out of this sum he was exempted from the payment of Rs.25,00,000 because the Company retained possession of the trans-Beas portion of Kulu and Mandi. This is how the Governor-General describes the transaction in his letter, dated 14th March, 1846, to the Secret Committee:

> It is highly expedient that the trans-Beas portion of Kulu and Mandi with the more fertile district and strong position of Nurpur and the celebrated fort Kangra—the key of the Himalayas in native estimation—with its districts and its dependencies should be in our possession. These provinces lie together between the Beas and Chukkee Rivers and their occupation by us will be attended with little cost and great advantage. . . . In consideration of the retention by us of the tract above described a remission of 25 lakhs from the crore of rupees which Rajah Gulab Singh would otherwise have paid will be allowed.

Of the 75 lakhs, 50 lakhs were to be paid on ratification and 25 lakhs before the 1st October, 1846. The Maharajah had considerable difficulty in finding this large sum in cash. Of the 75 lakhs the British Government was already in possession of 15 lakhs, being the treasure of Suchet Singh buried in Firozepur which on the death of that chief the British Government had refused to hand over to the Lahore Durbar on the ground of there being another claimant in the person of Gulab Singh. This sum of 15 lakhs was accepted in part payment of the indemnity charged to Gulab Singh.

Though Gulab Singh became by this treaty the Maharajah of Kashmir he was not yet in possession of it. It was only its legal title that was transferred to him. Wazir Lakhpat, who was sent to Kashmir to take possession of the country from the Sikh Governor, found it no easy task. Sheikh Imam Uddin, the Sikh Governor,[1] acting on the instructions of Rajah Lal Singh, the Minister of the Lahore Government, refused to surrender the province. After some trouble the Wazir seized Hariparbat, the fort that commands Srinagar. But as his position was critical the Maharajah sent him reinforcements under Wazir Ratanu. The Sikh army of occupation attacked the Maharajah's forces. Wazir Lakhpat was killed and the small force sent to take

[1] Sheikh Imam Uddin is described as follows by a contemporary in an article in the *Calcutta Review* of July, 1847: 'The Sheikh is perhaps the best-mannered and the best-dressed man in the Punjab. He is rather under than above the middle height, but his figure is exquisite, "as far as it goes," and is usually set off with the most unrivalled fit which the unrivalled tailors of Kashmir will achieve for the Governor of the province. His smile and bow are those of a perfect courtier whose taste is too good to be obsequious; his great natural intelligence and unusually good education have endowed him with considerable conversational powers.'

over the country was itself in imminent danger. Moreover, rebellion broke out at the instigation of the Lahore Durbar in the province of Rajouri and Rampur. Faiz Talib of Rajouri, who had cherished the feud to which his father had fallen a victim, was specially active in raising a rebellion. Gulab Singh was sorely beset on all sides. Wazir Ratanu was holding out in Kashmir, but he had already been reduced to desperate straits. The Maharajah then called upon the British Government to give him possession of Kashmir, as he had fulfilled his part of the contract. Dewan Jwala Sahai, his Chief Minister, was sent to the British Government to press this point of view. He was received by the Governor-General, who undertook to help him in getting possession of the territory and sent Colonel Lawrence to assist him. The Sikh Government was called on by the British to compel their Governor to yield the territory, and Lal Singh was forced to send an army against his own agent. Sardars Tej Singh, Sher Shah, Mangal Singh, and Generals Kahan Singh Man and Lal Singh Moraria were asked to proceed to Kashmir. This force marched through Bhimber. A small British force led by Lawrence also marched into Kashmir.

The Jammu force was under Maharajah Kumar Ranbir Singh. Colonel Edwardes also joined the

Maharajah at Reasi. Sheikh Imam Uddin was informed of the view of the British Government. When he was thus forced by the united authority of the British, Lahore, and Jammu Governments he surrendered personally to Lawrence. He declared then that he had acted according to the written instructions of Lal Singh, and proved his *bona fides* by producing the Purwana of the Wazir. On this the British Government required the dismissal of Lal Singh from the control of affairs at Lahore.

With the surrender of Imam Uddin, Kashmir and its dependencies passed quietly into the hands of Gulab Singh. The Maharajah entered Srinagar on the 9th November, 1846.[1] Imam Uddin had left two days before and in order to avoid a meeting with him the Maharajah made a détour on his route. He entered Shergarhi at 8 a.m.

In 1847 the tribes of Hazara rose in rebellion. Dewan Hari Chand, who was sent to put down the rebellion, was unable to cope with it. Finally, Dewan Jwala Sahai himself had to go, and he succeeded in suppressing it. The Maharajah, however, decided to ask the British Government to exchange Hazara with Mandir and Garhi which had been given as jagir to Captain James Abbot for

[1] Report of Lawrence to Sir Frederick Currie, dated 12th November, 1846.

his services in marking the boundary lines. Negotiations were opened for this purpose and Jwala Sahai was sent to Lahore to negotiate the agreement. After much preliminary conversation an agreement was signed by which Hazara was assigned to Lahore and the Jammu boundary between Muazaffarabad and the town of Jhelum became the River Jhelam.

The Maharajah by this received Kathua and Suchetgarh with part of Minawar. The boundary was further altered in 1847, when the State handed over the district of Sujjanpur and part of Pathankot in lieu of an annual payment to the disinherited rajahs of the hilly districts who took up their abode in British territories and to whom the Maharajah agreed to pay a perpetual pension amounting in aggregate to Rs.62,200 per annum. The most important of these pensioners were the Rajahs of Rajouri, Jasrota, Ramnagar, Besohli, and Khistwar.

By the second Treaty of Lahore the Sikh Government was for the time placed under the complete control of Sir Henry Lawrence, and through his intervention the agreement was signed on the 5th May, 1847. The settlement of the boundary between Tibet and Kashmir was entrusted to Vans Agnew and Alexander Cunningham. They left Simla on the 2nd August, 1846. Nothing was done during the year and Cunningham was again sent with Henry Strachey and Dr. Thomson. The boundary as it now exists was fixed by them.

New troubles arose in connection with other areas within the State. The district of Poonch had originally been given to Rajah Dhyan Singh by the Lahore Government as a fief. On the death of Rajah Dhyan Singh and his eldest son, Rajah Hira Singh, the jagir was confiscated by the Lahore Government on the ground that the holders died in rebellion against the State. It was then conferred on Faiz Talib Khan of Rajouri. When the area between Ravi and the Indus was given in sovereignty to Gulab Singh, Poonch also passed to him. The Maharajah then conferred it on Jawahir Singh, the eldest remaining son of Dhyan Singh. Jawahir Singh now put forward a claim to Poonch as the Raj of his father, to Jasrota as the jagir of Hira Singh, to a part of the income of Kashmir, and to a share in Gulab Singh's private property on the ground that they were the joint family property of all the brothers. He and Moti Singh also claimed that they should be included by name in the Treaty of Amritsar. The matter was referred to the British Government and the Maharajah deputed Jwala Sahai as his agent. It came up first before Henry Lawrence on the 11th August, 1847. Through Mohur Singh, who represented Jawahir Singh,

Lawrence advised the Mian to come to Lahore and have a personal interview with him. The Mian, however, hesitated. He was peremptorily asked to go to Lahore on the 3rd January, 1848. The Mian put off the appointment on the ground that there was an earthquake which was inauspicious. Jawahir Singh was really playing for time. He was hoping that Lawrence, whose friendship for the new Maharajah was well known, would not continue at Lahore. This happened as he wished, and when Sir Frederick Currie was appointed Resident the Mian came to Lahore and placed the matter before him. The matter was submitted to arbitration and an agreement was effected. Jawahir Singh and Moti Singh were given two jagirs, Chalayar and Watala, with the title of Rajah. They were to give to the Maharajah one horse with gold trappings every year and they were bound to consult him in all matters of importance. Their claim to be included in the Treaty was dismissed as being preposterous. The following are extracts from Sir Frederick Currie's judgment, dated 12th May, 1848:

> That whereas the rights, titles, and interests in the hilly countries possessed by the Sikh Government passed into the hands of the British Government and whereas in pursuance of the provisions of the treaty executed by the

latter with the Maharajah Sahib Bahadur, all these rights, titles and interests in the said hilly country have been completely and absolutely transferred to the Maharajah Sahib Bahadur and whereas it is incumbent to maintain the old and established rights of all rightful persons it is directed that the Mian Sahibs will have no power or authority to dispose of in their own holding any important matter without personal consultation with and advice of the Maharajah Sahib Bahadur.

And the Maharajah Sahib Bahadur is assured that the entire administration of the whole country whether in the possession of the Maharajah Sahib Bahadur or his officers shall remain the Maharajah's sole concern.

Jawahir Singh and Moti Singh quarrelled in 1852, when the matter was again referred to the Punjab Government, who awarded Poonch to Moti Singh as a jagir on the same conditions.

Jawahir Singh fell into the hands of an intriguing adventurer, Maulvi Mazar Ali, whom he appointed his Dewan. The Maulvi was sent to Swat to recruit an army, but the British authorities stopped him and he was expelled from the Punjab. Then Jawahir Singh personally went to Colonel Lawrence and asked that he should be made independent. His intrigues and disloyalty having come to light his estate was confiscated.

It will be remembered that the treaty of 1846 included Chamba but excluded Sapti as the territory of Gulab Singh. The Rajah of Chamba claimed Bhadarwah, which had been granted to him as jagir by Ranjit Singh, and as by the 5th Clause of the Treaty of Lahore the British Government had agreed to respect the *bona fide* rights of the jagirdars in the territories transferred to it, the Rajah of Chamba's claim to Bhadarwah was strong and unimpeachable. But the position was anomalous, inasmuch as Chamba had been transferred to Gulab Singh and Bhadarwah, which was within the geographical limits transferred, was the possession of the ruler of Chamba. The matter was settled by the arbitration of Henry Lawrence, who awarded Bhadarwah to the Maharajah, together with Lakhanpur and Chandgraon, while Chamba ceased to be a part of the territories of Jammu and Kashmir and became a State in subordinate alliance with the British Government.

The State thus assumed its present shape. An area consisting of more than 80,000 square miles, including part of Tibet as well as a part of the Pamirs, besides the genuinely Indian kingdoms of Jammu and Kashmir, came into Gulab Singh's possession. This area had never been effectively united under one ruler before and much of it, with, of course, the exception of the Valley of Kashmir, had never known settled government. The work of acquisition was finished. The work of consolidation and of government remained, and this, in view of the diversity of population, interests, climate, and lack of continuity in the past, was by no means an easy task. It is to the great credit of Gulab Singh that to this all-important task he now bent his energies, and though he was already fifty-three when he became a Sovereign Ruler, his efforts in this direction were crowned with success.

CHAPTER VIII

THE REIGN OF GULAB SINGH

THE State that was thus created differed from the other internal States of India in that it was independent in its internal affairs. No control was exercised by the British Government in the administration, and no Resident was appointed. In fact, the political position in the Punjab made any such intervention impossible. The hostility of the Sikh population and the strained relations with Afghanistan made it necessary for the British Government to cultivate the friendship of Gulab Singh and to treat him as a specially valued ally. If at any time they had other ideas, the crisis to which affairs in the Punjab were fast moving showed them in which direction their true interests lay.

1848 saw the outbreak of the second Sikh War. Sardar Chattar Singh allied himself with Dost Mohammad Khan, and the whole of the Punjab rose up in arms against the establishment of British authority in Lahore. Chattar Singh sent an agent to the Maharajah at Srinagar, but Gulab Singh advised him against his schemes. Dost Mohammad also sent an agent, but the Maharajah refused to receive him. At the beginning of the war Gulab Singh wrote to the Government of India expressing his readiness to help. The Simla authorities were in a suspicious mood and even thought that the Maharajah was not to be trusted. But when the situation became serious, Gulab Singh was requested to help the British by closing the passes and to despatch an army to fight the rebels. The boundaries of Kashmir were closed and a strong force under Syed Ghulam Ali Shah and Wazir Zorawar was sent to Lahore with instructions to act under Sir John Lawrence's orders. The Maharajah also kept three divisions at Munabir, Bhimber, and Mirpur to prevent the rebellion from spreading to his territories.

An attempt was made by Sir Lepel Griffin at a later time to connect Gulab Singh with the second Sikh War. He says: 'Although the proofs of Gulab Singh's complicity in the rebellion might fail to satisfy a court of law, yet there is sufficient evidence for history to decide against him.' What this evidence is that Sir Lepel Griffin considers to be sufficient for history will be seen from his views given below:

> In the first place, there is the universal belief, shared by the late Dost Mohammad Khan, that Gulab Singh was the instigator

> of the rebellion and that against his will Chattar Singh would not have raised his hand. The evidence given by Hiranand, the agent sent by Chattar Singh to the Maharajah, recorded in October, 1849, though in many parts exaggerated and contrary bears the general stamp of truth. . . . No documentary evidence of any kind was discovered; but the most wily of men was not likely to commit himself by writing what might be verbally explained, or expressed by a sign or by the pressure of a finger.[1]

This is the evidence which the imagination of Sir Lepel considers to be sufficient for history to decide against Gulab Singh. It consists of a common belief, which it is said was shared by Dost Mohammad, and is merely rumour. In the circumstances of the rebellion it was clearly to the advantage of the rebels to spread the rumour that the powerful sovereign of Kashmir was going to join them. The friendship with Chattar Singh, the second piece of evidence, does not mean anything. The Maharajah maintained friendly relations with almost all the chiefs at the Sikh Court, and to infer from it that none of them would have 'raised his hand' without the approval of Gulab

[1] *Punjab Chiefs*, Second Edition, p. 511.

Singh is obviously absurd. The third point on which Sir Lepel Griffin makes his allegation is the deposition of Hiranand, the agent of Chattar Singh, which definitely tries to implicate the Maharajah. But Sir Lepel himself agrees that his evidence is exaggerated and contradictory. Why it should be believed only when it goes against Gulab Singh does not seem clear.

Griffin, writing two generations after the event, wishes to implicate Gulab Singh in the second Sikh War on no evidence, while we have the evidence of Sir George Clerk,[1] who, writing in March, 1849, immediately after the rebellion, stated that he had tried very severely the loyalty of Gulab Singh on many occasions and found him true.

In fact, Gulab Singh did everything in his power to help in the suppression of the rebellion, as we have pointed out above.

The strength of the Sikh army was broken at Gujrat, where Ram Singh met an heroic death. Says the author of *Gulabnama:* 'Ram Singh Chuppuwalla, who was very brave, not likely to run away from the field, drank very boldly of the cup of death and proved the manly valour which he possessed.'

When Lord Dalhousie came to Lahore, Gulab Singh was invited to go down and meet him. He

[1] *Life of Sir Henry Lawrence,* Third Edition, p. 388.

came down from Srinagar to Jammu but did not go to Lahore. The Maharajah had good reasons for avoiding the interview. It was well known that Lord Dalhousie not only disliked Gulab Singh, but carried his prejudice to the extent of quarrelling with Sir Henry Lawrence on that account. The Commander-in-Chief, Lord Napier, however, fixed a day for a visit and they met at Sialkot. Sir John Lawrence came to Jammu to escort the Maharajah to the meeting place. Another attempt was made by the Governor-General to meet the Maharajah. It was suggested that he should visit Jammu, and Dewan Jwala Sahai was sent to settle the ceremonials. As no agreement could be reached with regard to the formalities of a visit to Jammu, it was finally decided that the Governor-General should come up to Wazirabad. The Maharajah, accompanied by the heir-apparent, Ranbir Singh, Rajahs Jawahir Singh and Moti Singh and other leading sardars went to Wazirabad. Sir John Lawrence, who was then the President of the Board of Control in the Punjab, came with Sir Robert Montgomery and Lord Napier to receive the Maharajah, who was accorded military honours.

The interview between the Maharajah and Dalhousie had to be postponed for a few days owing to the indisposition of the latter. When it actually took place the Maharajah was escorted to the camp of the Governor-General. Dalhousie himself came to the door and took the Maharajah by the hand and seated him on his right. Salutes were fired and presents were exchanged.

In 1850 Sir Henry and Lady Lawrence came to Kashmir by the Banihal route. They were received at Anantnag by the heir-apparent, Prince Ranbir Singh. During their stay at Srinagar they met Gulab Singh several times. Lawrence went from there to Skardu and Ladak. The object of his mission, of course, was to see what were the possibilities of the Central Asian trade.

European visitors had already begun to come in large numbers to Kashmir, and as early as 1847 Gulab Singh was complaining of their irregularities. Dr. Honigberger, who visited him in that year, records the following conversation with the Maharajah on the subject:

> At the period when I was in Cashmere the Maharajah had several English visitors whom he treated with the greatest hospitality. . . . In a conversation, however, which I had with the Maharajah, he complained that many of the servants of European visitors had abused the hospitality displayed towards them, for they had frequently taken with them very large quantities of saffron and other products of the

country, much beyond what they could really use during their sojourn.[1]

Among the prominent visitors who were the Maharajah's guests were Lord Grifford, brother-in-law of Lord Hardinge, Sir Henry Lawrence, and Colonel King.

In spite of the personal cordiality between the Maharajah and high British officials, diplomatic relations at this time were not wholly friendly. In 1848 Lord Hardinge wrote to the Maharajah stating that the nature of his internal administration aroused misgiving in the minds of the British Government, and claiming the right on the part of the Company to interfere in his affairs. The object of this communication was to get a Resident appointed at Srinagar, for which no provision had been made in the treaty of 1846. The Maharajah claimed that a promise had been given to him that no Resident would be appointed in his State. The matter was again raised in 1851 on the ground that every year there was an increasing number of British visitors to the valley whose interests should be looked after by a Resident. The Maharajah strongly resisted this claim, protesting that the appointment of a political officer, as in other Indian States, was

[1] Honigberger, *Thirty-five Years in the East,* pp. 178-179. (London, 1852.)

against the degree of independence guaranteed to his State, and that as the European visitors frequented the valley in summer it would be sufficient if an officer were appointed for the season only. On this, the Government of India withdrew the claim to appoint a Resident and agreed to the deputation of an officer in Srinagar for this duty during the summer only. The following letter from Sir John Lawrence, dated 14th January, 1852, to Dewan Jwala Sahai, will show the purpose of the appointment:

> On account of certain excesses committed by some European visitors in the past year, I intend to appoint some responsible European official at Srinagar to stay there till the return of the said visitors in order that he may put a stop to the occurrence of such excesses. As the Maharajah is well acquainted with the good intentions and sociability of Major MacGregor, I wish he may be allowed to stay at Srinagar till the end of the hot season to supervise the conduct of European visitors to Kashmir. As this arrangement is also for the benefit of His Highness it is hoped it will be gladly accepted by His Highness.

The officer so appointed enjoyed no powers of

political supervision. The proposal to appoint a Resident was revived in 1873, when Maharajah Ranbir Singh was on the throne. In a well-reasoned communication the Maharajah pointed out that there was no provision in the treaty which gave authority to the British Government to appoint a Resident, and quoted as a precedent the proposal of 1851. The British Government then withdrew the claim.

The administration of Kashmir called forth all the statesmanship of Gulab Singh. In the later days of Sikh administration the affairs of the province had been sadly neglected. The shawl industry, which is the mainstay of the population of Kashmir, was weighed down by heavy and capricious taxation; reckless Governors, especially Sheikh Imam Uddin, had given away much of the land in the valley as rent-free concessions; an oppressive system of begar, or forced labour, made the life of the peasantry miserable; sati and infanticide were common; the hilly areas were infested with robbers.

Almost immediately on taking up the reins of administration Gulab Singh determined to make his power felt through the length and breadth of his vast kingdom. He put down rebellion with a strong hand. Order was restored in every part of the country and every effort was made to render trade and commerce safe for all. The result was immediately visible. Nicholson notes as follows in his official Diary on the 19th November, 1847:[1]

> Had some conversation with a party of Kabul merchants taking tobacco and snuff to Kashmir whence they intend returning with *pattoo* and *tosh*, which last fetches a very high price in Kabul. They complained of the oppressive duties in their own and Maharajah Gulab Singh's territories but remarked that in the latter their goods were protected whereas they frequently ran great risks from the plundering tribes between Kabul and Peshawar.

The great difficulty that the Maharajah experienced was with regard to jagir grants. There were no less than 3,115 jagirs granted in Dharmuth besides numerous alienations of other kinds. A large number of them were unregistered. The Sikh Governors, Sheikh Goolam Mohi Uddin and Shiekh Imam Uddin, were extremely lavish in their grants, especially the latter, who for the sake of popularity signed away large tracts of land at the end of the Sikh régime. As soon as the Maharajah took charge of his country he instituted an inquiry of

[1] *Lahore Political Diaries,* vol. vi., p. 321.

quo warranto. The jagirdars and other grantees were greatly agitated and loudly complained that the Maharajah was resuming their ancient possessions.

Tyler, who conducted an independent enquiry, states[1] that the Maharajah was inclined to be just and reasonable. His point was that people who began as revenue farmers should not claim the land they held in farms to be jagirs; that grants when made should be strictly adhered to; that grantees who were given one acre should not be allowed to possess two on the same sanad, and that in cases of treason, rebellion, and gross misbehaviour the jagirs should be liable to resumption.

The question of begar, or forced labour, which was at that time widely prevalent and which caused the inhabitants a great deal of avoidable inconvenience, was also taken up by the Maharajah. His idea was to determine a certain number of men in each village who would be considered liable to do labour when called upon by Government. For this they were to be paid one kharwar of rice per month and their food when employed. Men not called upon to do begars in the course of the year were only to be paid six kharwars for the year. An officer was appointed to take charge of this work.

Another important reform undertaken by the

[1] *Punjab Political Diaries*, vol. vi., p. 60.

Maharajah was the rationing of rice in the valley. Kashmir, owing to its extreme inaccessibility and the insurmountable difficulties of heavy transport, was always liable to sudden famine owing either to failure of the rice crops or the cornering of the grain market. In order to meet this situation the Maharajah established a rigid monopoly of rice and had it sold at a fixed price to the people. Though this system gave rise to vociferous complaints, especially from the grain dealers, its wisdom was obvious. It is worthy of note that immediately after the recent Great War the State had to revert to this old practice of Gulab Singh and re-established the system of grain control.

Another serious question to which the Maharajah had to devote his earnest attention was the re-organisation of the shawl department.

The shawl department was carried on under a controller, who had under him the Nukdee karkhandars. A Nukdee karkhandar, or master of a factory, is in general a man of property. He has under him the shagirds, or workmen, whom he pays individually, and their materials are provided by him. He is responsible to the State.

Before 1833 the duty on shawls was levied according to the number made and stamped in the year at the rate of 3 annas in the rupee.[1] This was found

[1] Tyler's Report, *Punjab Political Diaries,* vol. vi., pp. 44-45.

unsuitable, and in 1835 General Mian Singh established the Baj, or fixed amount of tax, to be paid by each shop. The Baj was fixed at Rs.96 per annum and extended to 1,000 shops. This system was continued by Sheikh Ghulam Mohiudeen, though the tax itself was increased to Rs.120 per shop. When the Maharajah took over the administration he improved the system and renumbered the workmen.

For new shops Gulab Singh charged only half the tax for the first few years. In 1847 the karkhandars requested the Maharajah that there should be a yearly numbering of workmen, that the Nuzzerana should be reduced, that the wages of the workmen should be definitely fixed and that a settled Ayeen should be established for them. The other most important reforms that the Maharajah introduced as soon as he arrived in Kashmir were, firstly, the abolition of the Moulut, by which the accounts were continued to the 14th month, and, secondly, the cancellation of unnecessary taxes like the Chuttinia.

By the system which was in force the workmen were not free to change their masters. They were also paid very low wages; in fact, the wages which were fixed at Mian Singh's time were still in force when the Maharajah took control. When the Maharajah came to Kashmir complaints were heard that the karkhandars were not paying the workmen properly. He therefore raised their pay to 5¼ annas in the rupee, binding, at the same time, the workmen to do a fixed minimum of work.

On 6th June, 1847, the workmen struck work and about 4,000 of them set out for Lahore. The Maharajah told them that their complaints would be enquired into if they returned to work. This they did, and the Maharajah enquired into their case in open Durbar, and in July, 1847, promulgated a new system of control for the shawl department. By this the Kaid, or the law which bound the shagirds to work for the same master, was abolished and the workmen became free. The minimum salary for the workmen was fixed at 4 annas in the rupee, and the Baj system was abolished, the tax being imposed on the finished article. Very liberal arrangements were made for the Baj due to Government during the year.

The reorganisation of the shawl department was a great achievement, as the system had the following advantages:

(1) The baft system ensured that the tax should be regulated by the price of the shawl in market.

(2) The karkhandar had to pay only according to the work done in the shop.

(3) The shagird was no longer a serf.

These great administrative reforms restored the prosperity of the country, and Gulab Singh was in a position to devote his attention to the reorganisation of his army. The efficiency, contentment, and training of his forces were always matters of deep concern to him. As soon as he was established firmly on the throne he devoted his attention to these matters. Foundries and arsenals were established in the State; the forts were repaired and garrisoned; the hill levies, which formed his main strength, were organised into regiments, and a code of military instructions and orders was drawn up. It is of special interest to note that instead of copying English words of command the Maharajah had the same coined in Sanskrit. The names of his regiments were also taken from Hindu tradition. Thus there were the Gobardhan Regiment, the Raghunath Regiment, and the Lachhman Regiment. The military efficiency of his forces was recognised by all observers and stood the test of more than one difficult campaign on the Gilgit frontier. Indeed, events on this frontier took a critical turn soon after his accession. After the second Sikh War his attention was mainly devoted to troubles in that area. To a discussion of the course of events in that region we must now turn.

The Gilgit frontier occupies to-day a position of importance in the defence of the Indian sub-continent. But in the middle of the last century, when Russia was still far away from the Indian frontier, no importance was attached to this hilly country on the roof of the world. The area on the northern and western sides of the Indus has long been under the occupation of independent and unruly Mohammadan tribes. These tribal communities, who are often at feud with one another, acknowledge no master. The most important among them are the tribes in the Khushwaqt country, whose chief is now the Mehtar of Chitral. Other important chiefs are the Mirs of Hunza and Nagar, and the Rajah of Punial.

In 1841 this frontier witnessed one of those sudden convulsions which are not rare in tribal communities of a warlike character. Gaur Rahman, the eldest son of Mulk Imam, the ruler of Yasin, and brother-in-law of Imam-ul-Mulk, the Mehtar of Chitral, attacked and conquered Gilgit and killed its ruler. Karim Khan, the brother of the dead Rajah, thereupon called upon the Sikh Governor of Kashmir for help. The Sikhs, not loth to extend their territory into Central Asia, deputed Syed Nathu Shah of Gujranwalla, a capable commander, with a strong force to the help of Karim Khan. In 1842 Astore was occupied by Nathu Shah and Gaur Rahman was defeated. Though recalled for a short time, during which Gaur Rahman inflicted a defeat on the Sikhs, Nathu Shah was sent back again, and successfully pacified the border, taking in marriage the daughters of

Gaur Rahman, and of the Mirs of Hunza and Nagar. Karim Khan, who had asked for Sikh aid to get himself restored, received nothing. Gilgit was permanently occupied by the Sikhs.

When Gulab Singh acquired Kashmir, though the Treaty of Amritsar gave him only the hilly country between Ravi and the Indus, it was understood that he had inherited all the claims that the Sikh Government had over these areas. Nathu Shah also transferred his services to Gulab Singh and was entrusted with the Government of the frontier.

In 1847 Nathu Shah, with the permission of Gulab Singh, allowed Lieutenants Agnew and Young of the Bengal Engineers to visit Gilgit. Among Agnew's other exploits may be mentioned the fact that, being refused permission by the chief of the place to enter Nagar territory, he wrote to the Mir that the British Government, knowing that Gulab Singh's conquest of Baltistan and Ladak had caused him to be looked upon with apprehension by the people of those countries, had sent him to reassure them.[1] The Mir of Hunza accused Nathu Shah of having allowed Europeans to come to the country, and on this ground attacked him. In the fight that ensued Nathu Shah was killed. Gaur Rahman, the stormy petrel of the Gilgit frontier,

[1] *Lahore Political Diaries,* vol. v., p. 297.

also rebelled at the same time, and the whole frontier was up in arms. The Maharajah, however, sent a strong force and peace was restored.

In 1851 the frontier rose again in rebellion. The Chilasis began plundering the possessions of the Maharajah in Hazara. As the Maharajah was then in Jammu and winter was approaching he confined himself to making preparations for a punitive expedition. A powerful force under Dewan Hari Chand, Colonel Buji Singh, Colonel Jowahir, and Dewan Thakurdas was despatched in the spring of 1852. As soon as the winter was over Chilas was surrounded and besieged. The fort of Chilas is placed in a naturally impregnable position and the Maharajah's forces found great difficulty in besieging it. The country is very barren and the army had to depend on provisions taken from Kashmir. These, however, were soon exhausted. Over 1,500 men died in the course of a few weeks. Colonel Buji Singh was seriously wounded. Confusion prevailed in the ranks, and, according to the author of *Gulabnama,* the soldiers were forced to eat 'the leaves of trees and barks of plants.'

The endurance of the Dogra soldier shone out under these trying circumstances. The Maharajah was at that time in very bad health and suffering from dropsy, and anxiety concerning the fate of his army on the frontier was having visible effects on him. But, even in that state of health, when the news of the dangerous position of the army before Chilas was conveyed to him, he ordered that preparations should be made for him to start immediately.

While these preparations were in progress the Court astrologer appeared before him and said: 'Your Highness, the fort has already been taken; the soldiers have plenty of food and drink.'

The Maharajah, who was furious at what he considered to be an untimely jest, said: 'You have eaten well, but my soldiers are hungry and dying. How shall I trust in your word?'

The astrologer replied: 'If I am a Brahmin and the legitimate son of my father you will hear the news soon.'

The astrologer did not wait. He went home. The prophecy turned out to be true and the Maharajah was pleased and granted him jagirs which his descendants still enjoy.

The story of how the Dogra army, which was put to such straits, conquered the Chilas fort is interesting. The fort is on a high hill, and its water supply depends on one well. The Dogra commander ordered a big hole to be made and drained all the water from the well. Thus deprived of their only source of water the Chilasis surrendered. Their leaders were brought to Srinagar, where they accepted the Maharajah's authority and left their sons as hostages.

Hostilities were not, however, confined to Chilas. In Gilgit also trouble soon broke out. The Kashmir forces on the frontier were posted at three points: at Gilgit, at Bunji, and at Astore. The main force at Gilgit was under Bhup Singh. Gaur Rahman surrounded the two forts at Bunji and Astore. The garrison, which made a sortie, was cut up, and Bhup Singh's reserve, which was sent in relief, was totally destroyed. Of Sant Singh's main force at Astore only a Gurkha woman escaped. This brave lady threw herself into the river which flows below the Gilgit fort and, swimming across the Indus, arrived in Kashmir to tell the mournful tale. She was rewarded with a pension by Maharajah Gulab Singh.

In 1851 troubles arose on the Tibetan frontier also. The trade missions from Tibet were by old custom, which the Maharajah had undertaken to maintain, entitled to free transport. The Zamindars of Ladak, no longer afraid of the Tibetans, refused to render the mission free service. The Grand Lama protested against this breach of the agreement and deputed two Garpons, or Provincial Governors, to settle the question. The following is a translation of the agreement which was entered into by the representatives of the Maharajah and the Dalai Lama in this connection:

> This is dated the third day of the month of the Water Bull Year [apparently 1852].
>
> The Ladakis refusing to supply the Tibetan Government trader Ke-Sang Gyurme with the usual transport animals on account of the decreased tea trade, the Nyer-pass of the Garpons were deputed to enquire about this matter and to investigate the boundary dispute between Ladak and Tibet. A meeting was accordingly arranged between Ladak Thanadar Sahib Bastiram and Kalon Rinzin accompanied by his servant Yeshe Wangyal and an agreement was made as follows:
>
> In future the Ladakis will supply the Tibetan Government traders with the usual transport requirements without any demur. The joint Te-Jis[1] will request their Government to appoint only intelligent and capable men to take the annual tribute to Tibet. The Ladakis shall provide the Tibetan Government traders with accommodation and servants as usual and render them any further assistance according to the old-established custom. The Garpons

[1] *i.e.*, the Garpons of Sartok. 'Teji' is a Tibetan title which the then Garpons might have held.

will issue orders to the effect that tea and woollen goods arriving at Nagari shall only be sent to Ladak and not to any other place. The boundary between Ladak and Tibet will remain the same as before. No restriction shall be laid by the people of Rudok on the export of salt and woollen goods and the import of barley flour and barley. Neither party shall contravene the existing rules and the rates of Customs duties and market supplies shall be fixed by both parties concerned. The above rules shall apply also to the Rongpas[1], who export salt. The travellers from North and West who come through Rong are given passports by the Thanadar. They are liable to Customs duties as prescribed in their passports. Should any of them be unable to produce his passport, he shall be made to pay fifty times the amount ordinarily recoverable from him. No case will be heard against such recoveries made by the Customs Officer. In deciding all important matters the ruler shall take into consideration the manners and customs of both sides and observe the old-established rules regarding supply of transport, etc. There shall be no restriction in grazing animals in the pasture reserved for the animals

[1] *i.e.,* people inhabiting the valley countries.

> of the Government traders, but the people shall not be allowed to abuse this privilege by bringing animals from outside to graze on it. Both parties shall adhere strictly to the agreement thus arrived at between Tibet and Singpas (Kashmiris), and the two frontier officers shall act in perfect accord and co-operation.
>
> Drawn in duplicate and sealed by Thanadar Sahib Bastiram and Kalon Rinzin Two Nyerpass of the Garpons. Witness Yeshe Wangyal, Private servant of Kalon Rinzin.

We have already described the adminstrative reforms of Gulab Singh. His methods were no doubt medieval, but he took great pains in governing the country justly. As Sir Henry Lawrence has said, his government was 'mild, conciliatory, and even merciful.' He himself personally looked into all affairs, great and small.

An English writer who knew the conditions of the State well has thus described Gulab Singh's method of administration.

> He was always accessible and was patient and ready to listen to complaints. He was much given to looking into details so that the smallest thing might be brought before him and have his consideration. With the custom-

ary offering of a rupee as Nazar anyone could get his ear; even in a crowd one could catch his eye by holding up a rupee and crying out, 'Maharaj, Arz Hai,' that is, 'Maharaja, a petition.' He would pounce down like a hawk on the money, and having appropriated it would patiently hear out the petitioner. Once a man, after this fashion making a complaint, when the Maharaja was taking the rupee, closed his hand and said: 'No, first hear what I have to say.' Even this did not go beyond Gulab Singh's patience; he waited till the fellow had told his tale and opened his hand, then taking the money, he gave orders about the case.[1]

The Maharajah suffered from dropsy for a long time and had proposed to Dr. Honigberger that he should enter his employment and stay in Srinagar as his physician. The doctor, however, was unable to stay. The disease became worse with time, and in 1856 Gulab Singh's health began to fail. As a result he decided to entrust the administration to his only surviving son, Ranbir Singh, and to retire completely from the affairs of this world. In February 1856, he formally installed Ranbir Singh on the gadi and himself accepted the position of

[1] Drew, *Jammoo and Kashmir Territories*, p. 15.

Governor of Kashmir, and left for Srinagar to lead a quieter life. But even in the seclusion of Srinagar he was rudely awakened by the news of the great Indian Mutiny. As soon as this news reached him, though he was on his death-bed, he ordered Dewan Jwala Sahai to proceed immediately to Rawalpindi and offer all the resources of the State to the British Government in his name. He was specially ordered to offer free hospitality to all European women who might like to leave the plains. The offer of military and financial help was accepted, and Maharajah Ranbir Singh, together with Dewan Hari Chand, was ordered to go with a large force to help in the siege of Delhi. This was the last public act of Maharajah Gulab Singh. Soon afterwards his illness became worse and he died on the 25th Sawan, 1914 (Samvat), or August, 1858, at the age of sixty-six.

CHAPTER IX

CONCLUSION

It will be seen from what has been said in the preceeding pages that Gulab Singh was one of the most remarkable men that India produced in the nineteenth century. There had been others in the eighteenth century, such as Haidar-Ali and Maharajah Scindia, who, beginning their life in obscurity, founded kingdoms and dynasties. But his is the only case in nineteenth-century India where a man beginning as a petty official in a Court conquered kingdoms and territories and established himself as a Sovereign. In a century barren of political achievement in India Gulab Singh stands out as a solitary figure of eminence.

This is not his only claim to India's recognition. He is the only ruler in India's long history who could be said to have extended the geographical boundaries of India. His conquest and annexation of Ladak, which we have described in a previous chapter, is an achievement which writes his name for ever in the history of India. No previous Indian ruler, not even Samaudra Gupta or Akbar, had even dreamed of invading Tibet; and though Zorawar, who ventured too far, paid the penalty for his adventure, the Maharajah's forces routed the Tibetan army and extended the border of India to the other side of the Himalayas.

It is not claimed that the Maharajah achieved these results by methods which were always beyond criticism. Gulab Singh was no saint, and where his interest required he did not hesitate to resort to tricks and stratagems which would in ordinary life be considered dishonourable. He was trained in a hard school, where lying, intrigue, and treachery were all considered part and parcel of politics.

He was undoubtedly an opportunist, ready to stand out boldly or to withdraw as the occasion demanded, not committing himself irretrievably without making sure of his ground. He was willing to yield with grace when there was no other course open; to negotiate when that was suitable, even to part with money when that would serve his purpose. He was not one of those who rushed to arms at the first quarrel. As a skilful commander and a good soldier he knew that war was only the arm of policy, and he would not embark on conflict unless he was certain of success. Though he was chary of coming out into the open field on his own behalf, his courage was never in doubt. His brilliant defence of Lahore in the face of Sher Singh's army, his ride in the face of heavy fire at Multan, and numerous other instances given in the previous chapters, prove this. But he had great faith in his diplomatic skill, and it was on this, rather than on his army, that he depended for the success of his plans. At the same time it is recognised even by his enemies that he was not worse than others at the Lahore Court. Captain Cunningham, to whom Gulab Singh's name was anathema, says:

> In the course of this history there has, more than once, been occasion to allude to the unscrupulous character of Rajah Gulab Singh; but it must not, therefore, be supposed that he is a man malevolently evil. He will, indeed, deceive an enemy and take his life without hesitation, and in the accumulation of money he will exercise many oppressions; but he must be judged with reference to the morality of his age and race and to the necessities of his own position. If these allowances be made, Gulab Singh will be found an able and moderate man, who does little in idle or wanton spirit, and who is not without some traits both of good humour and of generosity of temper.[1]

Sir Henry Lawrence, who knew Gulab Singh intimately, formed the following impartial estimate of his character:

[1] Cunningham, *History of the Sikhs*, p. 332.

> I have no doubt that Maharajah Gulab Singh is a man of indifferent character; but if we look for perfection from native chiefs we shall look in vain. Very much but not all that is said of him might, as far as my experience goes, be so of any sovereign or chief in India. He has many virtues that few of them possess —viz., courage, energy and personal purity. . . . The way in which he has been doubted, denounced, and vilified in anonymous journals is very disgraceful to us.[1]

In fact, Sir Henry Lawrence stood so firmly by him that he did not even hesitate to quarrel with the Governor-General on this account. Sir Henry's defence of Gulab Singh ruffled the temper of Lord Dalhousie and led to a heated controversy which was finally set at rest only by the Governor-General's letter of 18th February, 1849, in which it was agreed to treat the question as a matter of honest difference of opinion.

Sir George Clerk, who had also unique opportunities of knowing Gulab Singh, held the same view.

That he was noble and generous will be conceded by all who read his life carefully. He rewarded his servants liberally; the grants and jagirs

[1] *Life of Sir Henry Lawrence,* Third Edition, p. 389.

that he gave to all who served him bear witness to this even to-day. That he was able to inspire loyalty and confidence in men like Jwala Sahai, Zorawar Singh, Dewan Hari Chand, and others, who were devoted to him until death, shows what hold he had on men. In spite of his intense selfishness, he remained loyal at heart to the Lahore Government. He had, it will easily be granted, sufficient justification for the lukewarmness which he exhibited towards the Lahore Durbar, but when they went to war he remained at their side, and even Cunningham agrees that what Gulab Singh would have liked at the conclusion of the war, even more than an independent principality, was to remain as the Vice-Regent of Dhuleep Singh. It was only when the intrigues of Lal Singh made that altogether impossible that he turned to the alternative of independence.

His justice was rude, but it was expeditious. He toured his State often, and was relentless in his punishment of corrupt and tyrannical officials. His summary methods in dealing with them made him a terror to the tribe of petty functionaries.

Gulab Singh was of a very religious bent. He remained an orthodox Hindu at the Sikh Court, where, if he had followed the example of Khushal Singh, he could have gained greater favours from Ranjit Singh. Numerous are the temples he built in Jammu. He undertook many pilgrimages, visiting almost all the holy cities of the Hindus in Northern India, including Gaya, Prayag, Benares, and Muttra. He was so orthodox that he prohibited the killing of cows through the length and breadth of his State. On his death-bed he distributed over Rs100,000 in antya dan, or last gifts of charity.

On the whole, Gulab Singh led a pure life. The Court of Ranjit Singh was dissolute in the extreme, and the Sikh ruler did not hesitate to exhibit himself in public in a drunken state. The morals of the Lahore Durbar were such as to shock even a corrupt age. But Gulab Singh was not given to these excesses. For the age and the circumstances of his time he led a life which could in no sense be considered dissolute.

Gulab Singh knew well enough the value of gold in such unsettled times and considered great expenditure on palaces and buildings to be mere waste of money. He has left no monuments that are artistically worthy of him.

In appearance Gulab Singh was highly distinguished. A contemporary who was not biassed in his favour says: 'In manner Gulab Singh is most mild and affable; his features are good, nose aquiline, and expression pleasing though rather heavy. Indefatigable in business, he sees after everything himself; hardly able to sign his name he looks after his own accounts and often has the very grain for his horses weighed out before him."[1] He was free, humorous, and intimate with all classes of his subjects. Even Major Smyth, who was violently prejudiced against him, states:

> With all this he was courteous and polite in demeanour and exhibited a suavity of manner and language that contrasted fearfully with his real disposition.[2]

Another authority, who knew him well, gives the following description of Gulab Singh as a soldier: 'Still with all this he must be accounted the very best of soldiers, and for an Asiatic and an unlettered and uneducated man, he is an able, active, bold, energetic, yet wise and prudent commander. He is anything but strong-headed and hot-blooded—prudently making slow but resolute and judicious movements; thinking more of his resources and reserves than most of his countrymen are wont to do. Looks more to the future, its wants and requisites, than either to the present or past. Slowly goes on and feels his way as he goes—always ensuring supplies and resources; quick in taking oppor-

[1] *Punjab Adventurer,* chapter xiii., p. 75.
[2] Smyth, *Reigning Family of Lahore,* p. 257.

tunities, fond of the defensive though ready to take the offensive when opportunity offers or requires—always considering arms as his last resource."[1]

The strength of will, the deep insight into human affairs, and the persistence with which he held to his objects are such as to deserve admiration. His ideas of administration were, of course, primitive, but he was essentially the type of man who conquered and welded together kingdoms, and not one whose greatness lay—as in the case of his son—in administration. But his achievement as a statesman was by no means insignificant. He succeeded in establishing peace and settled government in an area which, excepting for Kashmir, had never known it from the beginning of history. The hilly province which is now known as Jammu consisted of numerous petty principalities, each ruled by a rajah whose pretensions were no doubt great but whose resources were indeed small. To have united all these under a single Government, to have reduced Baltistan and Ladak, and to have held his own in the political field against the trained diplomatists of the East India Company, go to show that as an historic personality dominating the stage of contemporary events Gulab Singh had few equals in his time.

The Court of Ranjit Singh contained many re-

[1] Quoted in Smyth, *Reigning Family of Lahore*, p. 259.

markable men: the valiant Hari Singh Nalwa; Dina Nath, the Colbert of the Punjab, of whom it was said that his sagacity and far-sightedness were such that 'when the historical sky was clear he could perceive the signs of the coming storm'; Aziz-ud-Din, the courteous and polished Foreign Minister; Jamadar Khushal Singh, the Lord Chamberlain; and Attar Singh Sindhanwalla, head of a powerful clan and himself a noble, courageous, and chivalrous warrior; and not the least of all, Rajah Dhyan Singh; but all of them acknowledged Gulab Singh as their superior in statecraft and wisdom. It was only when these statesmen were replaced by the minions of Rani Jindan that Gulab Singh lost his influence at the Court; but even Jawahir Singh and Lal Singh had in their turn to depend upon the ruler of Jammu. When Ranjit Singh died Gulab Singh was easily the most influential person in the Sikh kingdom, and though the genuine Sikh sardars, like the Sindhanwalla and Attari chieftains, did not trust him, they recognised his loyalty to Ranjit Singh and his family, and his ability to control the affairs of the State. One who could be acclaimed as their leader alike by Aziz-ud-Din, Dina Nath, Attar Singh Sindhanwalla, and others who never saw eye to eye with him, was surely no ordinary man. The same may be said of the English statesmen who came into contact with him. With the

Lawrences he formed a lifelong friendship. Sir Frederick Currie, Lord Napier, and all others who had to deal with him considered him a courageous foe, a loyal friend, a wise and far-seeing statesman.

It would not be right, of course, to judge him by the standards which we now apply to leaders of men, but if we take the moral and political standards of the time, Gulab Singh may well be said to have been not only a great but also a good man. He was intensely pious, devoted to his family and friends, and never given to oppressing people or pursuing his enemies with vengeance. His religious foundations in the State are many, though not as numerous as those of Ranbir Singh.

Thus, when everything is considered, Gulab Singh will appear as one of the few great Indian figures of the nineteenth century, one who in his ambition even as a youth dreamed of states and kingdoms, whose iron will neither domestic calamity nor personal humiliation could bend, and whose physical and moral courage, tried on many a battlefield and many a crisis, won for him a throne and a place in the Valhalla of India's great men. The present Jammu and Kashmir State is his monument. As long as that exists his name will have a place in the memory of men.

APPENDIX I

Letters from the Governor-General to the Secret Committee, dated 14th March, 1846

It will be seen by the draft of Treaty now forwarded that, in consequence of the inability of the Lahore Government to pay the sum stipulated as indemnification for the expenses of the war, or to give sufficient security for its eventual disbursement, the Hill territories, from the Beas River to the Indus, including the provinces of Kashmir and Hazarah, have been ceded to the British Government.

It is not my intention to take possession of the whole of this territory. Its occupation by us would be, on many accounts, disadvantageous. It would bring us into collision with many powerful chiefs, for whose coercion a large military establishment at a great distance from our provinces and military resources would be necessary. It would more than double the extent of our present frontier in countries assailable at every point, and most difficult to defend without any corresponding advantages for such large additions of territory. Now, distant and conflicting interests would be created and races of people, with whom we have hitherto had no intercourse, would be brought under our rule, while the territories, excepting Kashmir, are comparatively unproductive, and would scarcely pay the expenses of occupation and management.

On the other hand, the tract now ceded includes the whole of the Hill possessions of Rajah Gulab Singh and the Jammu family. Its possession by us enables us at once to mark our sense of Rajah Gulab Singh's conduct during the late operations, by rewarding him in the mode most in accordance with his desires, to show forth as an example to the other chiefs of Asia the benefits which accrue from an adherence to British interests, and to meet the expenses of the campaign, which we declared our determination to exact, and which, excepting by the cession of territory, the Lahore Government is not in a condition to afford.

Rajah Gulab Singh has engaged to pay the crore of rupees demanded from the Lahore State, on being put by us in possession of the territory ceded by the 4th Article of the draft Treaty, on such terms and conditions as we may approve.

It is highly expedient that the trans-Beas portion of Kulu and Mandi, with the more fertile district and strong position of the Nurpur and the celebrated Fort Kangra—the key of the Himalayas in native estimation—with its district and dependencies, should be in our possession. These provinces lie together, between the Beas and Chukkee Rivers, and their occupation by us will be attended with little cost and great advantage. The Chukkee River in the Hills will hereafter be our boundary to its source and thence a line drawn to the Ravee River, and along its course, and across the Chenab to the snowy ridge on the confines of Lahool. This line will be laid down by officers sent for the purpose according to mutual agreement and will be accurately surveyed.

In consideration of the retention by us of the tract above described, a remission of twenty-five lakhs from the crore of rupees, which Rajah Gulab Singh would otherwise have paid will be allowed, and the Rajah will pay the remaining seventy-five lakhs, of which fifty lakhs are to be made good at once, upon the ratification of the Treaty and the remaining twenty-five lakhs within six months from that date.

Of the remaining portion of the territory ceded by Article 4 of the draft Treaty, the greater part, with the exception of the Provinces of Kashmir and Hazarah, is already in the possession of Rajah Gulab Singh and his family, for which he had been bound hitherto to render military service to a small extent to the Lahore Government and to present annually a horse, with gold trappings, as a heriot to the State.

The conditions which may be stipulated with Rajah Gulab Singh and the Treaty to which he may be admitted, will be reported in my next letter. Those conditions will be so drawn as to bind us to the least possible interference in his affairs, consistently with the maintenance of our paramount position over the Rajah and his country.

APPENDIX II

A Note on some of the Chief Officers of Gulab Singh

Dewan Jwala Sahai

Dewan Jwala Sahai, C.S.I., who was associated with the Maharajah from his early youth, was the son of Dewan Amir Chand. Amir Chand entered the service of Gulab Singh and served him faithfully on numerous occasions. It was mainly owing to his exertions that the siege of Reasi by Dewan Chand was raised (see Chapter II.). When Gulab Singh was made Rajah of Jammu in 1823, Amir Chand was elevated to the position of Madar-ul-Maham. Amir Chand died in 1836. He had three sons, Jwala Sahai, Hari Chand and Mihal Chand, all of whom achieved great distinction under Gulab Singh. On the death of Amir Chand, Jwala Sahai became the Maharajah's chief officer, which position he continued to hold till 1865. Under Ranbir Singh he retired from the post of Prime Minister of the State as a result of paralysis. Owing to the Maharajah's constant absence from Jammu on military expeditions, the duties of administration fell mainly on Jwala Sahai. He was the Maharajah's confidential agent in all diplomatic business and was mainly responsible for the negotiations in connection with the transfer of Kashmir. For this service he was granted extensive jagirs and a Rasum of Rs.4 in every 1,000 on all State income in perpetuity. Among his other achievements may be mentioned the liberation of Gulab Singh from imprisonment at Lahore in 1845, the arrangement with regard to the boundary question in collaboration with Major Abbot, and the settlement of the Poonch troubles. As mentioned before, he continued to serve the State even after the death of Gulab Singh.

Dewan Hari Chand

Dewan Hari Chand was mainly employed in military expeditions. After the death of Zorawar Singh in Tibet he was sent to reconquer Ladak and to meet the Tibetan invasion. He was successful in both, and the Tibetan Treaty bears his name. In 1845, when Jammu was besieged, he was put in charge of the main forces, and it was to him the Maharajah handed over charge of the city when he himself accompanied the Sikh army to Lahore. After the Treaty of Amritsar the Dewan was sent on many important expeditions—notably to Hazara, where the tribes had risen in revolt. He was also sent to Gilgit. When the Mutiny broke out and Maharajah Ranbir Singh was sent by Gulab

Singh to the help of the British at Delhi, Hari Chand accompanied him. He died during the campaign.

Wazir Zorawar

Wazir Zorawar, who earned undying fame by his conquest of Ladak and his invasion of Tibet, was a native of Kussal near Reasi. He began his career as a private soldier at Reasi. Being energetic and brave and well acquainted with the country round about, he came under the notice of the Commandant, who sent him with messages to Gulab Singh. On one such occasion he brought to the notice of the Maharajah the waste occurring in the Commissariat Department and placed before him a scheme by which considerable saving could be effected. Gulab Singh, who was quick to appreciate merit, accepted his proposal and entrusted him with the task of carrying out the scheme. He was so successful in this that he was soon raised to the post of the Commandant at Khistwar. The history of his campaigns has already been related.

Zorawar was remarkable among his contemporaries for his absolute financial honesty. He never accepted a present from anybody, and whatever was given to him was sent to Gulab Singh. He carried this principle to such a length that he only wore the clothes that the Maharajah gave him and was content always with a very meagre salary. He had another peculiarity. He never used to send despatches of any kind about his expeditions. The tributes and revenue collected were sent down post haste to Jammu, and the Maharajah had to discover from it what new country his general had conquered. By these conquests he and his family did not benefit to the extent of a single penny.

Colonel Basti Ram

Colonel Basti Ram, who was one of Zorawar's chief officers in the conquest at Ladak and the expedition to Tibet, was a Rajput from Khistwar. He accompanied Zorawar in his first expedition and was present on the occasion of the surrender of Skardu. He was one of the few who survived the disaster in Tibet. He was then made Commandant at Zanskar, where he greatly distinguished himself. Afterwards he was appointed Governor of Ladak and the Tibetan expedition. His chronicle appears as a part of Cunningham's *Ladak*.

Wazir Lakhpat

Wazir Lakhpat was originally the Chief Minister of the Rajah of Khistwar. When that principality was conquered by Gulab Singh, Lakhpat was taken into his service. He was sent on many important military expeditions and served his master well. In

1846 he was sent to take possession of Kashmir and to quell the resistance of Sheikh Imam-ud-Din. The Wazir took possession of Hariparbat but was killed in a subsequent action. He was a very loyal and competent officer of the Maharajah.

Nathu Shah

Nathu Shah was a Sayed of Gujranwala. He was the Sikh Commandant on the Gilgit frontier and was mainly responsible for the reduction of Junza and Nagar, the daughters of whose chiefs he married. When Kashmir was transferred to Gulab Singh, Nathu Shah accepted service under him. The visit of Vans Agnew to the Gilgit frontier in company with Nathu Shah alienated the frontier chieftain from him, and in the rebellion that ensued he was killed.

INDEX

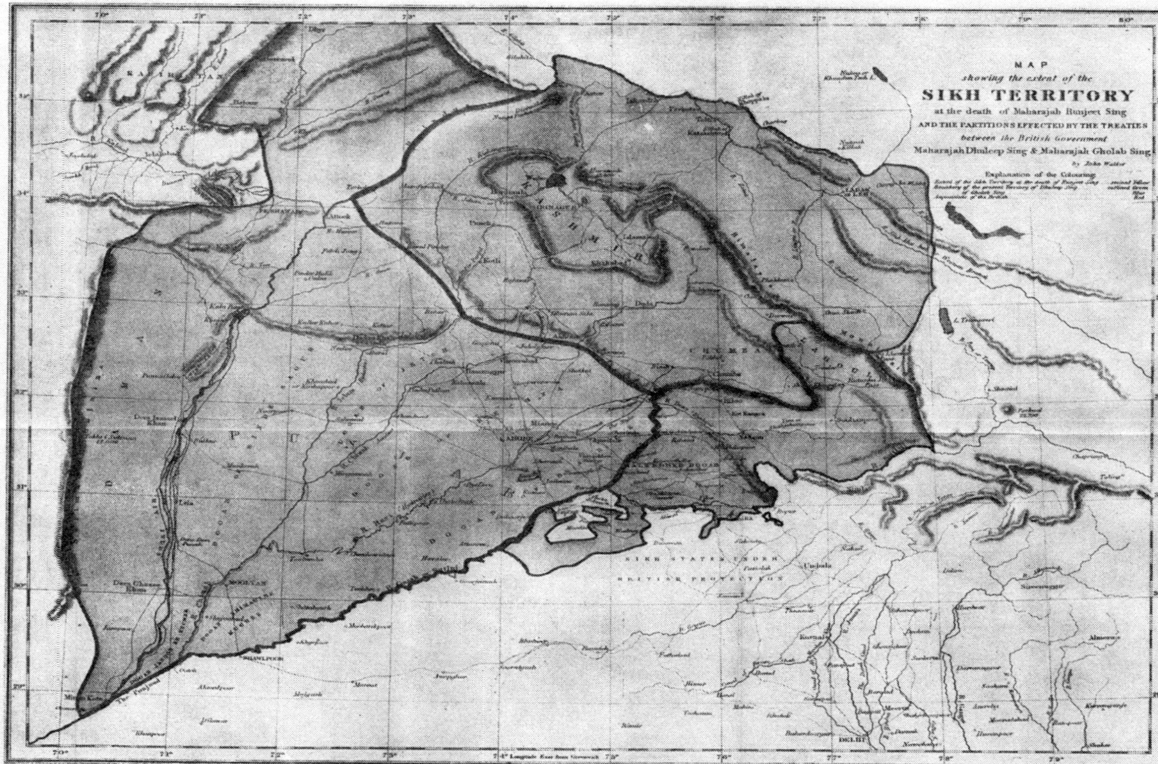
MAP
showing the extent of the
SIKH TERRITORY
at the death of Maharajah Runjeet Sing
AND THE PARTITIONS EFFECTED BY THE TREATIES
between the British Government
Maharajah Dhuleep Sing & Maharajah Gholab Sing
by John Walker
Explanation of the Colouring
SIKH STATES UNDER BRITISH PROTECTION
LAHORE
DELHI
MOOLTAN
BHAWLPOOR
Attock
Peshawur
Umbala
74° Longitude East from Greenwich